S0-BAR-712

Four French Organist-Composers

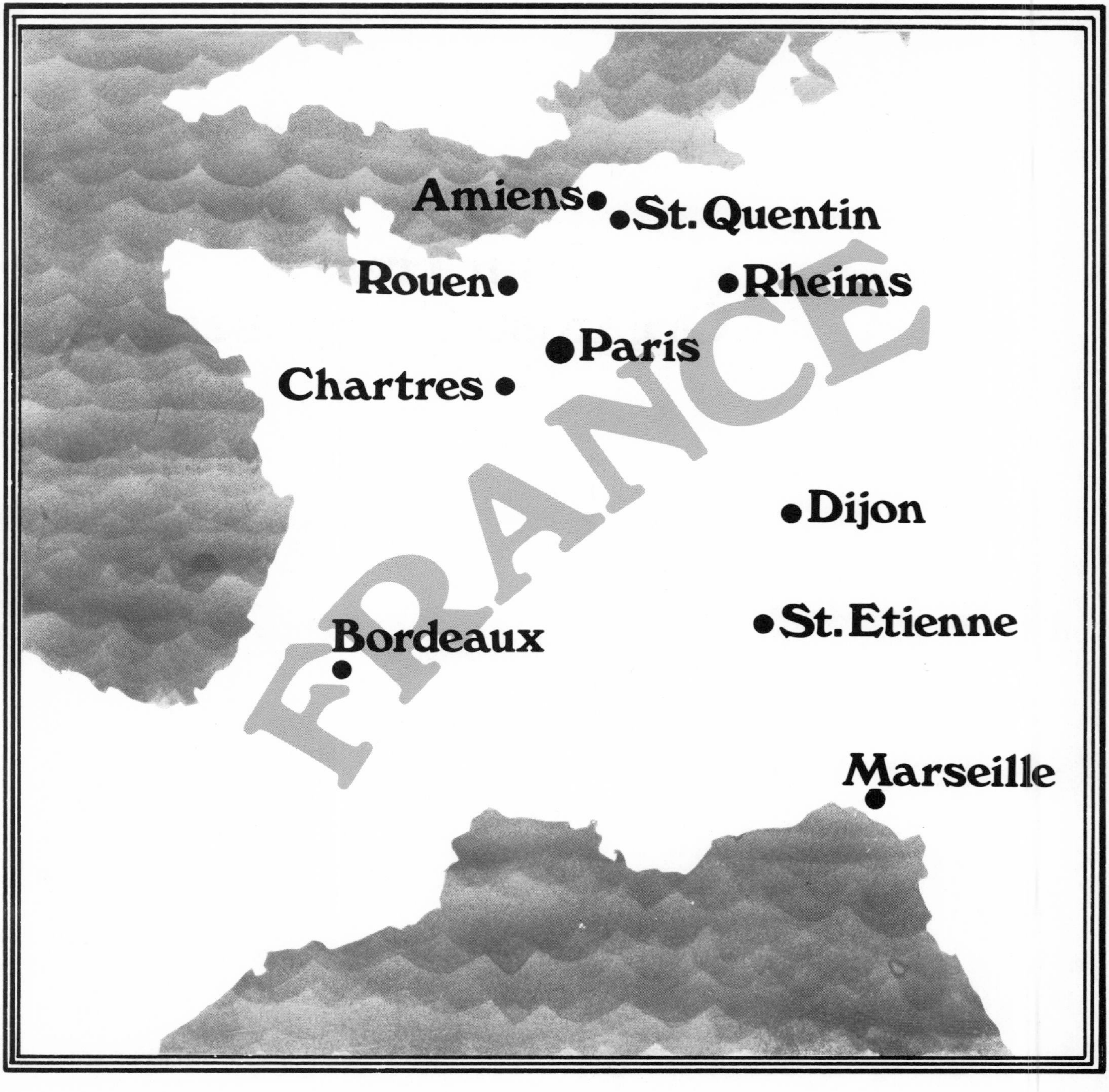

Amiens
St. Quentin
Rouen
Rheims
Paris
Chartres
FRANCE
Dijon
St. Etienne
Bordeaux
Marseille

Four French Organist-Composers, 1549-1720

by
Harry W. Gay

MEMPHIS STATE UNIVERSITY PRESS

Library of Congress Cataloging in Publication Data

Gay, Harry W 1925–
Four French organist-composers, 1549–1720.

Issued with phonotape (cassette, 2½ x 4 in.)
Bibliography: p.
CONTENTS: Introduction.—Titelouze, a beginning and an ending.—Multiple associations relative to André Raison.—Nicholas de Grigny, master at Rheims.—Saint Quentin and its organist Pierre du Mage.
1. Titelouze, Jean, 1563–1633. 2. Raison, André, d. 1719. 3. Grigny, Nicholas de, 1671?–1703. 4. Du Mage, Pierre, ca. 1676–1751. 5. Organ music—To 1800. I. Title.

ML390.G25 Phon Case 786.6D'2'22 74–34396

ISBN 0–87870–022–6

Grateful acknowledgement is made to the Bibliothèque Nationale, Paris, France for permission to reproduce numerous examples from their collection of organ compositions; the Bibliothèque municipale, Dijon, France for permission to reproduce "Le roi David et ses musiciens" from the Bible de saint Etienne Harding, abbé de Citeaux, Début de XII° siècle, (Bibliothèque de Dijon, ms 14, fol. 13 v°); "Music/The AGO-RCCO Magazine" for permission to reproduce three illustrations from the article, *Organs and organ building in France*, April, 1969 issue.

For Barbara Anne

Contents

List of Illustrations

Introduction

The object of this volume is to attempt to create a series of biographies drawn through the impressions of the author, but based, insofar as possible, upon research of available materials bibliographically presented, music composed by the men considered and on atmosphere created mentally through the absorption of history and of architectural considerations relative to the physical situations in which these composer-organists found themselves. From all this is deduced, in each case, a sketch of the *kind* of man who is being considered. Sometimes in showing that, or why, we may not know certain things, we discover some things that we may know as a result. It is hoped that this volume does not indulge fantasy to the extent of devastating facts, since the facts themselves are there as well. It becomes, therefore, a somewhat personal interpretation which could take, perhaps, some other form through some other hands.

The author wishes to acknowledge his debt to Félix Raugel and to André Pirro in freely paraphrasing certain basic materials. Expanded here, these materials, contrary to their indicated authors' original forms, have been documented in the Bibliography with sources, dates, translators and publishers.

In any discussion of the organ music of France, attention must be given to the important date of 757, the date of the arrival of the first organ in France. This seems to have been a present from the emperor of Byzantium to Pepin, King of France. This organ was set up in the royal villa of Compiegne. The next instance marking the installation of an organ of which we have record was that of the construction of an instrument at Aix-la-Chapelle in the year 826. From this time forward the use of the organ developed rapidly, and the number of instruments increased in accord with this demand.

To discuss the musical development of the country, one would have to begin with the famous Schola at Rheims. The history of this school dates to before the year 900. During the "reign" of Gerbert d'Aurillac, the Schola attained a very extensive reputation as a strict training institution. In determining the extensive use of the organ in the church and her services, one can cite the famous Bible of St. Etienne Harding. This Bible was completed in 1109 at Citeau under the direction of this learned man. In Tome III is found a very valuable illustration. This picture presents an imaginery impression of the City of God. King David is seated on a central throne holding a harp surrounded by various musicians. One among these musicians is an organist. He is seated before a keyboard of eight levers, and has depressed the keys d and f. This is very clear and there can be no mistaking the intentions of the artist. The details are so complete that the wind is generated by two series of bellows, and from these bellows, the wind is directed into the grooves under the pipes. It would seem, with this illustration in the Bible, that the organ was not only accepted in the services of the Church, but was highly regarded as well, and was an integral part of the worship. Of course, abuse was to be found, but in the main, the intent was one of a serious and dignified nature.

Pérotin – Baudoin and Jehan l'Organeur

Between the years 1180 and 1236, Pérotin le Grand was the organist at Notre Dame of Paris. There are still to be found in his extant works some trios which he had composed for use on the organ, or organs. Some of these either involved an organ of more than one manual, required the use of at least two organs, or were conceived for organ and one or two other instruments. It is rather more probable that these trios were performed in the latter arrangement, with the organ supplying only one of the parts. Next can be cited two organists who were trained at the Schola at Rheims. Baudoin l'Orgueneur and his son Jehan were famous in their day as performers on the instrument, and Jehan is remembered as an early composer. Both father and son were organists at the Cathedral of Notre Dame of Rheims during the reign of Philip IV. It was this King who, succeeding his father in the year 1285, supressed the power of the Papacy and the Order of the Templars and laid the strong foundations of a national monarchy. His was one of the most significant reigns in medieval history.

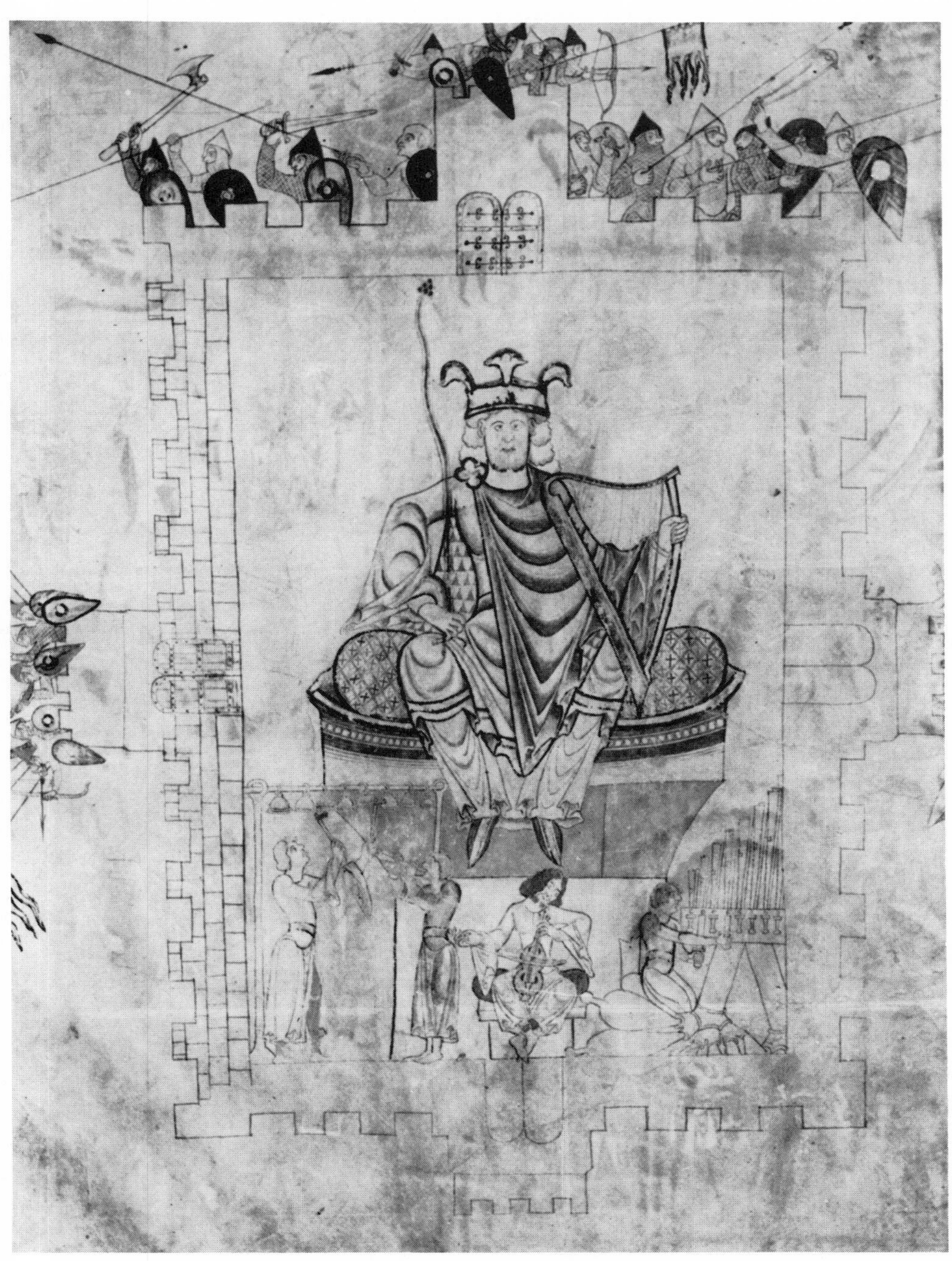

Detail from the Bible of Saint Etienne Harding, A.D. 1109 Ms. de Citeaux, Bible de Dijon, Nos 12-16.

''Le roi David et ses musiciens''

Machaut and de Vitry

Following the father and son l'Orgueneur at Rheims was the titan of medieval music, Guillaume de Machaut. After an extensive background cultivated in diplomatic service and by the travel involved in such service, Machaut decided upon a musical career and attached himself to the Cathedral at Rheims. He is credited with being the first to call the organ the "king of instruments". His writings contain numerous references to the uses of the organ in his day, and he even transcribed for the keyboard several of his vocal motets that they might be performed on the organ. Gabriel Zwick has pointed out the significance of the transcriptions of Machaut as well as the transcriptions of motets by de Vitry. He has presented these to us in modern terms and shows that both early composers were very definite about the use of the organ in the musical works attributed to them.

Indications of the Organ's Use

Indications of the obvious widespread acceptance and increasing usage of the organ are plentiful. These indications can readily be found in many descriptive sources in the writings of the times. In addition, the vital position held by the instrument can be determined by inspecting miniatures in manuscripts. Herein is found a veritable multitude of small drawings of organs and pipes. Embellished capital letters in hand copied manuscripts indicate in themselves a great consciousness of the role of this very popular instrument. Also an investigation of some of the fine stained glass windows of the thirteenth and fourteenth centuries will reveal the significance of the organ as related to the Church itself. Many instances of the appearance of the organ in sculptured decorations in the ceilings of great religious edifices are also to be found; and last, famous paintings have preserved for us a colorful source in fine detail of the existence and nature, in many cases, of the pipe organ. With so many sources available, we cannot help but be impressed by the interplay of this form of art with other phases of the greater area called Art.

de Zwolle and His Descriptions

Henri Arnault de Zwolle, organist and physician to the Duke of Burgundy, has given to us a very valuable account of organs in existence even before the time of Saint Louis. In his writings he described some very ancient instruments which were destroyed during his lifetime (flourished circa 1260). In addition to these descriptions, Arnault also preserved for us an excellent drawing of an organ which possessed manuals whose compasses were that of thirty-one notes. According to the drawing, the thirty-one pipes were distributed between two sidetowers with six pipes apiece and a flat center front. Also in the manuscript are found details of the construction of the mutation stops found on some of the organs. This manuscript (latin 7295) can still be inspected in the Bibliothèque Nationale.

Liber Organistoris and Henri de Saxe

From these descriptions, one would conclude that these organs had been in existence surely during the latter half of the twelfth century, reaching a termination in point of service sometime during the thirteenth century. During this same century, we might also call to attention the Liber Organistoris, a type of service manual used at Notre Dame de Paris. The real antiquity of this volume is easily determined from the writings of Henri de Saxe. On May 8, 1416, the Chapter of Notre Dame decided that this organist's guide for the services was so antiquated as to be no longer useful with respect to then current needs. This volume contained the organist's part of the service, notated in exactly the manner in which it was to be performed. These writings seem to indicate that this Liber had been used throughout the fourteenth century and perhaps even as early as the thirteenth century.

The official report presented to the Chapter on May 29, 1415, by the organist Henri de Saxe provides some interesting details with regard to the exact duties of the organist. In addition we can infer something concerning the role of the organ itself by the use made of the instrument in the services. Henri de Saxe indicates that the organist was to play at Vespers on the twenty-three feast-days found in the list given him. He was to play during the Mass for the Kyrie, the Gloria, the Sequence, the Sanctus and the Agnus Dei. In addition he was also responsible for certain repairs which might become necessary for the proper functioning of the organ. This amount of usage of the organ in the services indicates, in another manner, that the organ was a much respected instrument and was a highly utilitarian device in the divine worship.

Some Early, Larger Instruments

Proceeding into the fourteenth century, it is interesting to note the construction of some very large instruments, primarily in the region called Normandy. The cathedral at Amiens, as early as the year 1429, possessed an organ containing over two thousand pipes. The construction of this large instrument certainly dated well back into the previous century. The gigantic front of this instrument may still be seen. Other cathedrals began the construction of organs in the latter part of the fourteenth century, completing them in the early fifteenth century. Among these cathedrals and churches might be named those at Strassbourg, completed in 1489, Perpignan, in use in 1504, one at Gnosse completed in 1508, another at Mans, 1531 and those of Saint Bernard de Comminges (1536), Chartres (1542-1551) and Notre Dame des Andelys (1573). The total span of time in the construction of these instruments mentioned above is at least a century.

Some Evolution of Organ Style

The enthusiasm for the organ spread throughout Europe together with the influence of those musicians who had mastered its particular technique. The peculiar features of style which distinguished purely vocal music from that music designed for the keyboards were recognized and explored. As a result, there gradually evolved a style which was uniquely suited to organ music and to other music written for the other keyboard instruments. The development of this style first began with the discovery of the technique of treating with much freedom the highest part of certain vocal motets transcribed for keyboards. Through the medium of this newly organized method of treatment, organists developed an art of ornamental and expressive variation which was to play an important part in the complete pattern of development and evolution of instrumental music. The earliest existing collection of keyboard pieces which could have been performed on the organ is known as the Robertsbridge Fragment. This collection dates from the fourteenth century. The volume contains only six works. Therein are found three very well developed transcriptions of motets. These were taken from Le Roman de Fauvel, and specifically are from the Tribum-Quoniam Secta and the Firmissime-Adesto Sancta Trinitas, manuscript pages xlii and xliii. These transcriptions are very valuable, since one can easily compare the original motets with the arrangements made by some unknown composer of the fourteenth century. It was during this same era that Machaut, de Vitry and Jean de Muris worked in all forms of music, both sacred and secular. These three men are reputed to have been the first to anticipate the future role of the chromatic scale.

A Chronology – Some Musicians from 1400-1633

At this place it might prove profitable to present a list of musicians of whose existence and work we have positive proof, and to indicate where available their approximate dates of flourishing. Beginning with two names already indicated, one would mention Baudoin L'Orgueneur and his son Jehan who were organists at the Cathedral of Notre Dame de Rheims at the time of King Phillippe le Bel (the fourth).

Following in approximate order of chronology are Renaud de Reims (d. 1415), Henri de Saxe (c. 1435), Jacques le Mol (c. 1458), Mangendre (d. 1504), Jehan Peu (c. 1508), Jehan Regnault (c. 1527), Jean Mouton (c. 1528), Loys Regnault (c. 1568), Henri Beranger (1570), Jehan des Grez (c. 1572), Jean Boullery (1572), Jean Doysi, Baptiste Collet, Anthoine le Roy, Noel Cybot (1522-1556), Jean Pathie de Cambrai (1530), Rogier Pathie de Cambrai, Noel de Vertemont, Jacques du Buisson, Anthoine de la Hage, Jehan Doublet (1531), Firmin de la Lyardiere, Fortis Pujol, Jacques Cellier (1580), Jean Dugue (1580), Guillaume Costeley (1588), Thomas Champion, Jacques Champion de Chambonnieres, Nicholas de la Grotte, Joseph de Chabanceau (de la Barre), Deslions, Marin de la Guerre, Henri du Mont, Etienne Richard, Charles Racquette, Gabriel Garnier, Jean Buterne, Jean Denis, and Jehan Titelouze (1563-1633). Those composers listed from Champion onward are more familiar and their dates are certainly well enough known. They span the years from 1567 (the birth of Champion) to the death of Titelouze as noted, and for several years thereafter, since some of these men lived even after the death of Titelouze. In addition to this general list, there will be listed, with but one exception, the organists who served Notre Dame de Rouen from the year 1399 to 1633.

Cybot and Cellier – His Sketches

Among the aforementioned musicians, special attention should be given to Noel Cybot and Jacques Cellier. Cybot enjoyed a highly successful career while organist at the Sainte Chappelle from 1522-1556. At first he enrolled there as a singer in the choir, and later he became the organist at this famous church. Of perhaps greater interest now is the fact that two chansons and a magnificat which were composed by Cybot were published by Pierre Attaingant in the year 1529. Jacques Cellier was the organist at Notre Dame de Rheims about the year 1580. Additional importance is due him for leaving for later generations a collection of drawings in ink which included such organ cases as those at the Sainte Chapelle

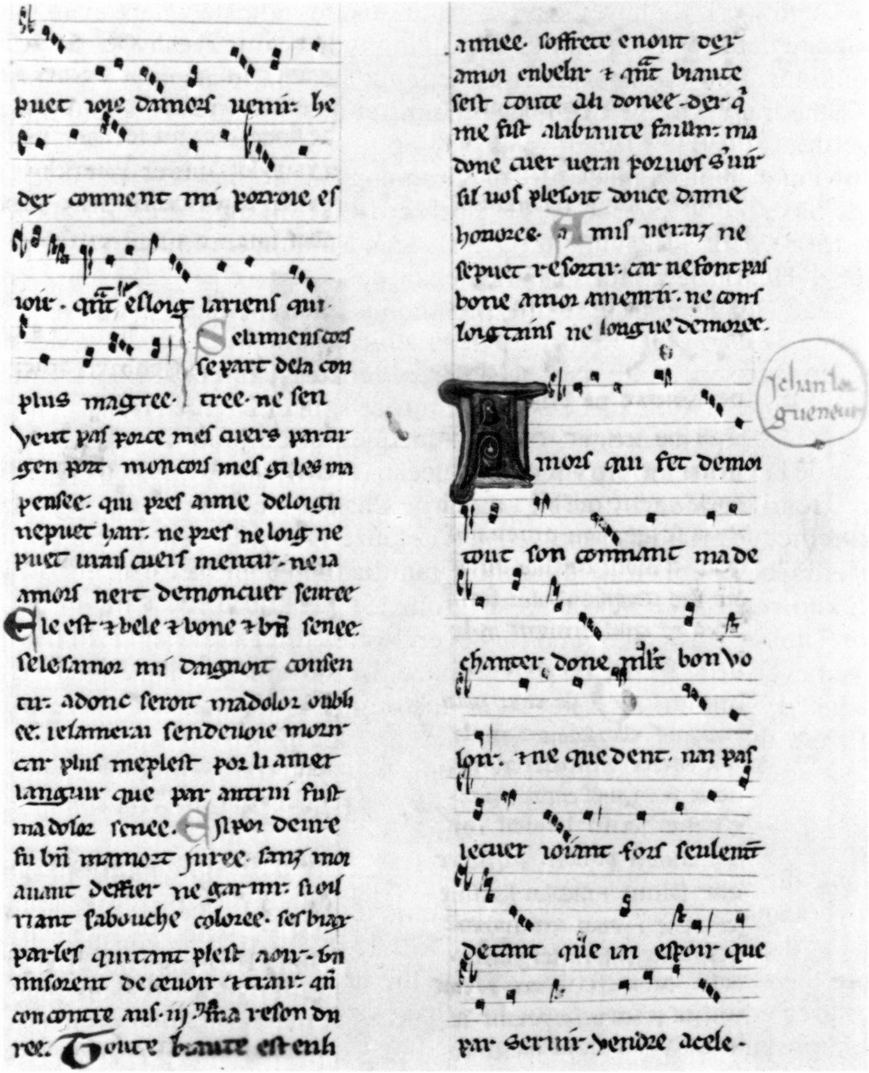

Chanson by Jehan, l'Orgueneur (Bibliothèque Nationale, Paris, Ms. fr. 845).

Organ tabulature by P. Megnier, copied in 1582 by Jacques Cellier, Organist of the Cathedral at Rheims.

and the Cathedral at Rheims. In addition to these drawings and sketches, he copied as well organ tablatures by Guillaume Costeley and de Megnier. These valuable works would have been lost but for this act of Cellier, and his copies are preserved in the National Library and are available for study.

The Instrument – 1400-1700

In any consideration of the organ music of France of this particular period, two factors must be considered as determining features of the type of music composed for the instrument. The first is the very nature of the instrument itself. French organs were never like those of other countries and still today manifest a distinctive national school of construction and voicing. When one reviews the literature of the instrument of this period, it is even more imperative that just consideration be given the even more peculiar design of the instrument as it appeared from 1400 to 1700.

To begin, let us recall the stoplist of an organ which, while not located within the political confines of the geographical boundary of France, still is an example of the very type of organ built in France. This organ is that located in Antwerp and built in the year 1394.

Open fluit (4′)
Rorefluit
Dulcian
Quintadeen
Sesquialter
Mixture
Regalis

The names of the stops vary from the French nomenclature, but the general principles of design are present. Again later, an organ built by Jean le Hourlier in 1537. This instrument was located in the church of Saint Germain da Chalons-sur-Marne. This organ is quite an advance over the work of the unknown builder of the Antwerp instrument. Its stoplist is as follows:

Principal de le pieds
Flûte bouchée de 6 pieds
Flûte de 1 pied et 1/2
Nasard de 2 pieds

Positif (sic) de 3 pieds
Fourniture a 5 rangs
Regale de 3 pieds
Tabourin de 6 pieds
Tremblant
Rossignols

As the last example of this earlier type of construction, it would be good to include the stoplist of the organ at the Cathedral of Troyes built in 1560.

Principal "de devant"
Octave du principal
flûte a neuf trous
nasard
cymbales
doucaine
fifre
hautbois et cornet
trompette

In the early formation of an organ ensemble no rule prevailed. In the fifteenth and sixteenth centuries, the stops were very full. One single drawknob would engage as many as ten, twenty or thirty or more pipes for each key. The great organ of this period in the Cathedral of Barcelona in Spain was noted for its magnificent twenty-seven rank mixture on the great organ. Each note on these organs set into vibration pipes of various lengths producing correspondingly varied pitches. The range of sound would include the speech of pipes from thirty-two feet to one-quarter of a foot. This multiplication of super-acute sounds was a source of damage to the balance of the voices. It was in this later period of the seventeenth century that after much study of acoustics, pipe construction and not the least of all, the composition of the music to be played on the instrument, the organ builders evolved the rules, so to speak, which still govern the construction of a rational organ as a musical instrument. Their problem of paramount importance was how to construct a mixture which would provide the necessary clarity to the ensemble without impairing the ability of the composer or organist to make intelligible a work of polyphonic proportions and design.

It would seem that earlier builders of this period resolved this problem by providing nine mixtures for those organs whose basis of tone was the sixteen-foot sound. For those instruments which had only the eight-foot stops as foundation, the builders provided seven mixture stops. To this principle and to the stops which had come down to these builders from the Middle Ages, the French organ builders added numerous other stops which were to play definite and directive roles in the literature of the organ. The reed stops of powerful proportions, the cornets, the stentorian mixtures, and the limited pitches of the pedals—all have this controlling effect upon the organ music of France.

Compositions of Specific Character

Perhaps it would be good to consider a few works by name to see in just what way these compositions would be relegated exclusively to the French organ of the day in which they were written. One of the first instances to note would be the general class of compositions entitled Récit de Tierce en Taille. This type of work historically calls for flutes of the sixteen, eight and four-foot pitches to appear on the swell organ as an accompaniment. On the choir organ the jeu de tierce would be drawn as the solo registration. This would include the eight-foot gedeckt, the four-foot blockflute, the two and two-third-foot nazard, the two-foot flute, the tierce and the larigot. In the tenor part, this combination gives some very rich overtones which penetrate the registration of the accompaniment and provide a setting of great color. The pedal should herein contain only eight-foot stops. An inspection of the stoplist of French organs of this period would show that the sixteen-foot stops were absent from the pedals. This arrangement allowed the primary polyphonic structure of many works to be presented on the manuals, and the plainchant theme to appear in the pedals on reed stops. Otherwise, the flutes in the pedals served to complete the scheme of accompaniment while the solo appeared on one of the manuals.

Another instance of the particular need for the French organ to play the music written by French composers is one taken from the first organ Mass of André Raison. As will be mentioned later when considering Raison, it is reasonable to conclude from the Qui Tollis of this Mass, even if no other source were available, that the organ which Raison played and for which this work was intended was one of four manuals. Herein there is a striking display of changing colors in rapid passages. This changing appears to be between the cromorne, the cornet and two sets of echo-type stops. When this piece is inspected and performed, it becomes obvious that this could be done, not with a personal stop manipulator, but through the use of four manuals.

Consider the work entitled Plein jeu by Louis Marchand. This work calls for four-part polyphonic movement on the great organ and for two pedal parts to be executed on the reed stops. Could one conceive this work on some organ other than one built to provide the means of expressing such a type of composition? This, and other such works of the period of music under discussion, fails in performance at the hands of so many present day organists who try to read from rather modern arrangements and play as the arrangements seem to indicate instead of in proper historical perspective. Then there are the ever obvious differences in design such as the inclusion in French organs of a Bombarde Organ with powerful reeds alone, or the use of the Voix Humaine in the French's own inimitable manner, or the Tambour and the Rossignol. Attention should be called to a very late installation from the point of view of all these considerations so far given. This is the great organ in the Church of Saint Sulpice reconstructed by Cavaillé-Coll in 1862. This magnificent instrument has twenty-six stops on the Great Organ. The pedal division is complete with twelve stops. Six of these ranging from thirty-two feet to four feet in length are of flute and string classes. The remaining six bear out the French tradition. They are reed stops within the limits of from thirty-two feet to four feet also.

Here the stoplist of the organ at Sainte Geneviève in Paris might do much to make this point final.

Grand Orgue:	Montre 16′	Double Tierce
	Montre 8′	Quarte de Nazard
	Bourdon 16′	Grosse Tierce
	Prestant 4′	Flageolet
	Bourdon 4′	Fourniture
	Flûte 4′	Cymbale
	Grand Cornet	Trompette
	Doublette	Cromhorne
	Flûte 2′	Clairon
	Nazard	Voix Humaine
Positif:	Montre 8′	Tierce
	Bourdon 4′	Larigot

	Prestant 4′	Fourniture
	Flûte	Cymbale
	Doublette	Cromhorne
	Nazard	Voix Humaine
Recit:	Cornet	Trompette
Echo:	Cornet	Voix Humaine
	Cymbale	
Pedales:	Flûte 8′	Trompette
	Flûte 4′	Clairon

This problem is very well expressed by C.F.A. Williams in reviewing the composition Kyrie on the First Tone by Raison. He has written that the piece begins with a dignified motive appearing on the plein jeu. The pedal enters later with the theme played on the trompette. His observation is that the piece ought to be very effective but it could not be played at all on a 3M English organ; for as he comments, if one were to couple the trumpet of the great organ to the pedal for the reed, it would render the great useless for the manual parts, and there would be no plein jeu. This is so since an eight-foot reed of trumpet character was practically unknown on an English pedal organ. This observation was made as late as the year 1905, and one can recall the nature of the English organ of 1700 to realize that this piece would not have been manageable at any rate on one English organ at that time.

The Church – A Controlling Factor

The other controlling factor which affected the type of music which the French organist-composer produced was, and still to a very real extent is, the organization which the composer served—the Church, that mystical body of Christ which so long had been the real source of new life for composers. It was in the confines of the service that the organist first drew his real inspiration to express musically those details of service which were needed for the glorification of God. Of the regulations which governed the organist, we might recall the Liber Organistoris mentioned earlier. This volume was used at Notre Dame of Paris from the thirteenth century. We know that the organist was told just what to play, as has been indicated earlier by the report of Henri de Saxe. A manuscript of about 1335 found in the Sagan monastery lists the parts of the service which were to be sung. These included the Gradual and the Alleluia verses. The manuscript adds however, that these were sung unless they were played on the organ. Even here was an indication of the later practice of alternative playing. Bartholomaeus de Glaville indicates in his writings of 1398 that the organ was used for the prose, sequences and hymns in the divine service. Much later, around 1662, the "Ceremonial de Paris" appeared to regulate the music of the services. During this extensive period the treatment of the organ in the churches was completely subordinated to the requirements of the liturgy.

Thus we see that the organist was told just when to play and nearly what to play in the services. Another aspect of this restraint is found when the time duration of the pieces is considered. These organ works were for a certain purpose and were required to fill a rather definite period of time. Therefore, we realize that the French composers of this period were limited in the lengths to which they could safely go in presenting music for a portion of the service. For instance a Kyrie movement could not conceivably last for five or ten minutes. The service would be protracted out of proportion to the requirements of the occasion if this and other such lengthy movements occurred during the Mass. The composers respected these limitations as can be seen by a study of the innumerable short pieces found published as movements in the Mass settings. It is true that there are some long works to be found, but the total number is so small as to be insignificant. These pieces are found primarily in the works of de Grigny and are not representative in any way of the total output of the composers of this era.

Plainchant – Its Force in Composition

In addition to these two phases of the problem attributed to the Church is a third and salient factor. This is the continued use of the plainchant. To use plainchant as a basis for composition, especially in religious works, had always been an accepted and respected practice. Yet the general musical activity of the Baroque Era was to supercede the ancient modal practices. The plainchant did not lend itself too well to the newer concepts of chromaticism as practiced by the composers who had come under the influence of the Protestant chorale. Consequently, we find, even until 1750 in France, the adherence of more or less faithful nature to the confines of the modes. Even with the genius of du Mage we find his writing a

"Suite in the First Tone". This continual fettering to the ancientness of the ecclesiastical worked as a stagnation to the composers who could produce a great quantity of works, but always within rather narrow limitations. It is a real tribute to the genius of the men whom we have chosen to discuss that they were able to write such works as they did, chained as they were to the invariance of tradition.

It seems almost incongruous when we realize that the practical ultimate in the use of the plainchant appeared with Titelouze, the earliest of the composers represented herein. From that time onward there seems to have been a real striving for something new, but eventually no better. A limited number of themes had been set in strict polyphonic fashion and seem to have had their musical potentials exhausted in one man. Hereafter are found solo settings, suggestions of themes, dialogues, récits and a number of other media of expression. It is true as indicated earlier that many of these later works were good and highly noteworthy, but the use of the chant was less learned in many ways.

It does not take much investigation on the part of anyone who can compose a little music to see just how difficult it is to supply genuine, sincere and inspirational counterpoint in providing an idiomatic keyboard composition upon a theme which is as limited as plainchant. Furthermore, it is almost as difficult to supply a work of harmonic proportions upon such a theme. One needs only to review works built upon such theme as written by Tournemire, Widor, Langlais, and Messiaen, to mention but a few of the twentieth century composers, to realize the boundaries within which a composer must work even today. Much of this type of music, regardless of the ingenuity evidenced in the writing, begins to sound very much alike after the fifth piece. The music becomes much like the theme—anonymous, traditional, obscure yet beautiful but of the same genre. This matter of the regulations of the Church posed a profound problem for the composers of this more ancient era of musical development.

It is within these particular confines that the composers of the organ music of France must be considered. The organ works which can be found in the archives which precede the date of the first publication of organ music in France, made by Pierre Attaingnant in 1531, are real experiments in just what could be done in the way of writing music which was particularly conceived for the organ. It is not to be supposed that these works themselves were successful in this experiment, but there was progress made in establishing the beginnings of an independent style of expression. If the works included in the Attaingnant collection are examined, they will be found to consist of compositions of scalar character in the right hand supported by hollow chords in the left hand. Others are efforts of severe contrapuntal nature with some built upon the plainchant. The striking feature of these works is that they are certainly designed for the keyboards. It is impossible to conceive that they could be performed as vocal works with any reference to the efforts to evolve a style for the instrument as opposed to transcribing for it from vocal scores. These works are monotonous, and this monotony is only concealed somewhat by the particular timbres of the instrument. Nevertheless, there was a pattern being evolved, a frame within which to work, in which a form of liberation was evident and the elements indicating the appearance of the fugue became apparent.

Claudin le Jeune

If we should choose to name those persons between the appearance of the anonymous authors in the Attaingnant collection and the end of the sixteenth century who made profound contributions to this immanation of organ style, three would suffice to span this space of time. From the standpoint of genius alone the name of Claudin le Jeune would head the list. This man was the composer of the King's chamber music. He wrote for the Church, even though he was a Protestant; and he was an uncontested master of French polyphony. His great contribution to the realm of organ literature development was his *Fantaisies instrumentales* for organ or viols. These were not published until twelve years after his death, in a volume of Mélanges published in 1612. Several of these fantasies have secular melodies or themes, while one is based upon a religious theme, the benedicta ex celorum. In this collection there is evidenced a new form for the instruments—the ricercare. This is exposed as a short prelude on a given theme which is then subdivided into a number of episodes which follow each other in fugal style. These works represent a new era in this process of development and expansion of a truly keyboard style.

Charles Guillet

The second name to be entered on the roster of those making real and original contributions to the solution of this posed problem is that of Charles Guillet. This musician flourished around 1654 and originally was from the city of Bruges. His was a type of theoretical work which included the composition of some twenty-four fantasies for the viols or the organ. These were published in 1610. These fantasies were composed in four parts, and along with them in the volume were examples of some elegance which were designed to aid those who wished to learn how to write instrumental and polyphonic music in the ecclesiastical modes.

This composer is noted for his use of chromaticism, which is encountered with some frequency. He seemed to know just how to provide the spirit of animation to a musical phrase by the use of well calculated rhythms, as exemplified in the fantasies seven, nine and fifteen. He also understood well the method of animating a phrase by the control of the volume of the melody as made evident in the third and twenty-second fantasies. Only once did he resort to the device of augmentation so well established by his predecessor, Eustache du Caurroy. This technique, which consists of doubling the value of the notes of a repeated subject, is found in the tenth fantasie in the sub-ionian mode. Throughout all his work Guillet seems often to have found a new form of expression.

Eustache du Caurroy

However, the works of the great Eustache du Caurroy seem to be the most successfully conceived possible adaptation to the organ. Caurroy was the canon of the Sainte-Chapelle du palais, and was several times lauréat du Puy de Musique d'Evreux. This man was a scholar, a theorist, an interpreter, and a composer possessing keen insight into the musical problems with which he dealt. Coupled to all these avenues of expression, and probably of greater significance at the time, is the fact that Caurroy was also the valet of the King of France. In his musical works as listed are to be found vocal motets, masses, songs, psalms, and a set of Fantasies for the organ. These pieces are in three, four, five and six parts.

These, as those of Claudin le Jeune and Charles Guillet, can be performed by an ensemble of instruments; but the basic design seems to have indicated rather well that the author had arrived at a place of detachment from other influences of style, and had realized that beginning of the end of the solution to this problem of providing organ music for the organ. Some of these fantasies adapt themselves extremely well to the organ. Others, those of five and six parts, sometimes seem a little dense in sound. The listener can easily become confused in listening and lose the thematic development. Nonetheless, when they are studied and known, they represent no more of a problem to us than any other work of somewhat complex proportions. These were most probably intended as a set of complete experiments in learning just how much could be expected from the arrangements for the organ.

One must consider that Caurroy had a magnificent instrument upon which to play these pieces. His was the organ which was represented in the ink drawings of Jacques Cellier. With such an instrument, things could be achieved in the way of sound which might prove impossible or unsatisfactory on some other instruments. Of the fantasies in three and four parts, the outstanding ones are those based upon the "Salve Regina" and the "Ave Maris Stella". In all these works the form used is that of the ricercare. However, within this outline of form, the composer devises each piece in a different way.

One of the usual devices which Caurroy uses is that of decomposing the theme into smaller segments and stating these segments in polyphonic settings before the entrance of the theme itself in notes of longer value. Thus the theme is broken into parts, and the parts become themes for each section of the whole. He is highly successful in this technique, as a study of the fantasie based upon the Noel "Une Jeune Fillette" will show. Some of these themes he used were borrowed from plainchant. In addition to the two mentioned above, one fantasie is composed upon the theme of the "Pange Lingua". Theoretically, Caurroy remained under the influences of the modes; yet, he was daring enough to allow certain dissonances, such as seventh chords which lead toward modern tonality, to enter and enrich his works.

These fantasies were not published until after the death of the composer. Even at that time they appeared in part books for solo instruments instead of in score, as would have been needed to demonstrate Caurroy's keyboard intentions. Today they are being edited for publication by this author in a reasonable form for organ performance. Perhaps three or four have made their way into anthologies; but here they are often distorted and the true meaning of the composer is not to be found. They are written on two, or at the most, three staves and are generally indicated to be performed upon some ensemble of stops instead of appearing with each part as a distinct linear feature in the polyphonic structure of the pieces.

For those readers interested in a transcription of one of the Mélanges (*Mélanges de la Musique de Eustache du Caurroy, Maistre de la Musique de la Chappelle du Roy*, published by André Pitard, Paris 1610) one such can be found in the famous *A General History of Music* by Charles Burney. His apparent disdain for the French musician is obviously exposed in a footnote. Certainly his study of the Fantasies was incomplete.

Possible Influence of Improvisation. Charles Racquette

Here then we gain a brief picture of the situation which existed in France from 757 until the work of Eustache du Caurroy. All would tend to point to a long history of the use of the organ in the services of the Church, and to some extent, in the secular works of the day. The unfortunate factor in all this information is that few of the actual compositions which were performed during this long period have come down to us in any manner of completeness. While we can read of this organist and that one as performers in various churches and cathedrals in the city and in the provincial areas, we are bound only to these remarks, since many of the works performed are not mentioned and are not available. It is possible that the French were then, as they are now, much given to improvisation, and that this form of musical expression took the place of many works. If the improvisations of the cathedral organists in France today were written down each time a new piece was executed, the volumes filled by such music would be a number such as to be unbelievable. Whether or not this was the fact of the matter, we are unable to determine.

A case in point in a later period might indicate the extent of training and musicianship with which French organists were endowed if the instance of the appointment of Charles Racquette be considered. When auditioned for the position as organist at Notre Dame of Paris, Racquette was instructed by Père Mersenne to execute extempore a work based upon plainchant. Racquette did this, developing a long fantasie which completely amazed his examiners. This work was later written down by the composer, and is still available in Raugel's published collection. One can readily see the real source of amazement when the composition is performed upon the organ.

However, if any discussion of the real music and the composers who have written it is to be undertaken, it will be necessary to consider those organists who lived and worked after 1563, the birth of Titelouze. To form the basis of this brief investigation into some of the organ music of France, I have selected for discussion four organists of different backgrounds, different locations, of varied methods of expression, and who were apparently unknown to each other.

TITELOUZE – A BEGINNING AND AN ENDING (1563-1633)

Some Influences

Joliet, organist at Chartres; Leroy, organist at Saint Omer; Jacques Lefèvre, organist at Saint Maclou; Joseph de la Barre, organist of the King; Florent Bienvenu, organist of the Sainte Chapelle; Nicholas Barbier, Crespin Carlier, Valerin de Heman, Guillaume Lesselier, Claudin le Jeune, Jacques Mauduit and probably Père Mersenne all are supposed to have climbed the steps of the platform of Notre Dame de Rouen to meet or hear the great exponent of French polyphonic art, Jehan Titelouze. Here was a man of much influence who served the Cathedral of Notre Dame from 1588 until 1633. In addition to the real musical service he rendered the Church during his tenure, he taught many students and attempted to imbue them with the same degree of technical understanding of the art field in which they had chosen to exert themselves as he had himself. He was many times called upon to inspect organs of various builders and to pronounce the final word of acceptance of them. He was in demand by builders themselves for advice upon voicing and the proper disposition of the registers of the organs. He was also called upon to provide stoplists for various organs to be constructed. Thus we read of his dictating the specifications for the organ of Saint Godard in Rouen just a few months before his death in 1633.

Failing Health and Death

About the year 1622 Titelouze began to be concerned about his state of health. We know that he had suffered, even before that time, a small period of depression. His doctors had advised him to go to the country at that time. Some time later he seems to have been obsessed by some fear. An incident of note could be inserted here. In order to get to the organ loft, it was necessary to use a small portable ladder. Guillaume Le Herpeur, the chief bell-ringer for the Cathedral, had the custom of borrowing a ladder, used by Titelouze to gain access to the organ loft, to ascend to the tower to ring the bells. When the bell-ringer died a little later from the plague, Titelouze informed his colleagues that he would not go up into the organ loft until they had purified by fumigation the stairway which led up to the instrument. So his fear for his well being was manifest in this concern that he did not become infected by this pestilential microbe. The canons did see to it that the stairway was aired and made as safe as they could do so, that the fears of the organist would be quieted and that he might return to his task at the console. He became ill again in 1626 and again in 1629. This latter stage of illness prevented him from making one of his rather frequent and enjoyable journeys to Paris. He was able again in 1632 to go again to Paris to see de la Barre and to meet his editor, Pierre Ballard. Upon returning, he planned to move as his doctors had earlier urged him; but he was confined to his bed shortly after returning; and after six months in a state of confinement, his fragile constitution could continue the battle no longer. His death came October 25, 1633.

The disposition of his body was almost foreordained. There was a natural resting place for one who had given so much of service and of himself to the cause of music and to the Cathedral. His devotion was such that in the year 1610 the Chapter had made him a canon; and for his continued devotion, the colleagues who held such admiration for him placed him in a tomb in the vaults which for forty-five years had been made to vibrate under the touch of his hands and feet on the organ.

Rouen Cathedral – Something of Its History

The Rouen Cathedral was first consecrated in 1036. Of this early edifice nothing seems to remain. There was another cathedral built after the year 1200 when there was an enormous fire which destroyed the whole of the church. There seem to have been some parts, however, which were earlier than this fire such as the Northwest Tower, the Tour Saint Romain and the two chapels of the chevet, those of the transept and part of the nave, and the two doors of the West façade opening on the side aisles. It is known from a letter of Bishop Hugh that work was in progress on the rebuilding of the Cathedral in the year 1145. At this time the lower story of the Tour Saint Romain with its octopartite rib vault seems to have been constructed. In 1175 it is believed that the upper story of the tower and the portals were completed.

On Easter Monday, April 10, 1200, the entire Cathedral was burned. With it were consumed its bells, books, records, and ornamental fixtures. It was at this time that the greater part of the whole city of Rouen was destroyed, including other of its churches. Responding quickly to the tragedy, the citizens cleared away the wreckage and began to rebuild the city; and as early as the year 1204, work was already begun anew on the Cathedral. Concerning the completion of this new edifice we are uncertain. It is known from church records that important ceremonies were held in the Cathedral in 1223 and that in the year 1235 Bishop Moritius was buried in the choir. It is therefore believed that this building was practically complete by about the year 1250. The two transept façades date from 1278. The Lady Chapel was built in the fourteenth century, the foundations for the Chapel being laid in the year 1302. In 1487, the Tour de Beurre was erected. This tower is so named because it was financed from offerings made for the indulgence of using butter in Lent.

Another smaller fire succeeded in damaging the central tower which was rebuilt in the year 1514. The iron spire with which this tower is now crowned is, however, the result of some reconstruction of the nineteenth century. Dom Pommeraye, seventeenth century historian of the Cathedral, indicates that the existing façade was most probably erected between the years 1509 and 1530.

Items of Architecture and Dimension

The whole structure of the cathedral is somewhat curious. There are many irregularities of design including the incorporation of the famous false triforium, the strange disposition of the real triforium, and certain round arches in the clearstory. There are some more fortunate features of the structure, nevertheless, including the details of capitals and moldings, and the full system of five shafts rising from the ground. The interior of Rouen is unfortunately not so satisfactory as the interiors of some other of the great French cathedrals. One is impressed by the rather unfortunate division into four stories and the lack of harmonious relations concerning the proportions. Yet the Tour de Buerre and the West façade are considered to be masterpieces of the great flamboyant style; and included in this is the famous chapel of Saint Jean Baptiste, which is supposed to be the earliest extant example of flamboyant architecture.

Concerning the dimensions of the building, the interior is four hundred and forty-six feet long and one hundred and six feet wide, the transept being one hundred and sixty nine feet. The height of the nave vault to the crown is ninety-six feet. Within the cathedral are tombs of two important sixteenth century cardinals dating from the Renaissance. The Tour de Beurre is two hundred and fifty-two feet high. The cathedral was seriously damaged in World War II, but has been restored and was reopened for services in June, 1956.

The Hysteria of Chartres Transferred

In all the construction which was necessary to gain a rather complete cathedral building, the era which saw the construction of the edifice built before the great fire of the year 1200 contains perhaps one of the most curious examples of the application of hysteria or fervent belief in all the annals of ecclesiastical history.

The events of this hysteria began at Chartres in 1144 in the construction of the cathedral there and spread the next year to almost all of Normandy. Some of the monks at Chartres noticed about this time a special veneration expressed by the people toward the Blessed Virgin. The monks constructed some carts, built in a special fashion in which were placed all manner of materials for the construction of the cathedral. The people, told that these carts were constructed in honor of the Virgin, then hitched themselves to the carts and dragged the materials to the place where the cathedral was being erected. The carts were of unusual size and became larger in the course of the application of the will of the people to do this task as outlined to them. This seemed to be a form of penance and the labor was voluntary and was entered into in a zealous manner.

An account of this type of activity is found in two important pieces of correspondence of this time. One is a letter written by Brother Haimon of the Company of Saint-Pierre-sur-Divers in Normandy to his fellow servants at the Tutbury Abbey in England. The letter is dated the year 1145. Another letter was written the same year by Hugo Bishop of Rouen to Bishop Thierry of Amiens. Both of these letters are concerned with the account of the witnessings of the sight of these carts being dragged about. Brother Haimon related that thousands of persons would be pulling the carts along. The wagons were filled with wines, grains, oil, stone, wood and all that was necessary for the wants of life. The carts progressed along the journey in great silence. Any occasion of stopping was only for the opportunity to say prayers and beg for pardon for sins committed. If any one was so unholy as to be so influenced by his sins that he could not forgive a brother, he was cast from the company and his share of the load on the cart cast off as unclean.

The priests had the task of exhorting to penitence all who were in this grotesque procession. After the procession had stopped and confessions had been made the priest assured the penitent that God had forgiven them; then the blessed ones would arise from their knees and move forward with their burden as though nothing could stop their progress toward the cathedral. When the procession reached the cathedral, the wagons were dragged into a circular array in the form of a pitched camp. Tapers and lamps were attached to the wagons. The infirm and sick were placed there along with the relics of the Saints for their relief. The workers would then celebrate most of the night with watches and canticles. The priests would conclude the service and would lead a procession in which all participants would follow with devout hearts, imploring the clemency of the Lord.

Other letters tell of the occasions of the priest's using a whip to aid the penitent ones to obtain pardon. Children, old persons, men and women alike were in these processions. It is told that they would reach their destination and would fall upon the ground to bite the dust and eat the earth in their state of exaltation. Others who had not experienced the feeling of the saving pardon of God would strip to the waist and lie on the ground imploring the priest to use the whip and to spare them nothing in the way of punishment to assist them in obtaining remission for their sins. So in this state of devotion, the populace of Rouen followed the pattern of the devout Christians of Chartres and contributed to the erection of the great edifice of the twelfth century—that which with its bells, books, records and ornamental fixtures was consumed by fire on April 10, 1200.

Cathedral Musicians Before Titelouze

Into the life and activity of a cathedral whose history dated backward so many centuries came Jehan Titelouze in the year 1588. He had been engaged as organist at Saint Jean, also in Rouen, in the year 1585; and three years later he was called to the organ at Notre Dame to replace the Abbé François Josseline, organist and organ builder. The position in which Titelouze found himself was one which dated back many years. It is good to consider the names of those illustrious organists who contributed so much to the making of the music heritage of Rouen. At Notre Dame in 1399 was the organist Robert Labbé. He was succeeded in the year 1403 by Colin Le Neuf. Following Le Neuf was Colin Crasbouel, appointed in 1414. He served until the year 1433. The name of the organist who served from 1433 to 1450 seems to be lost. However, in the latter year an organist by the name of Hersent was engaged and served until the year 1452. There begins an unbroken line continuing to the advent of Titelouze. The appointments are in order: Jacques Duval 1452-1457, Raoul Lefèvre 1457-1467, Jean Fleury 1467-1483, Robert Martin 1483-1488, Guillaume Duval 1488-1499, Raoul de Sceyne 1499-1512, Simon Leclerc 1512-1521, Pierre de Palude 1521-1524, Jacques Brunel 1524-1525, Nicholas du Lot 1525-1526, Simon Magdelain 1526-1539, Guillaume Montcuyt de Darnetal 1539-1560. At the conclusion of Montcuyt's tenure, Abbé François Josseline was appointed organist; and, as was indicated above, Titelouze was his successor.

Who Was Jehan Titelouze?

Who really was this man Jehan Titelouze, a man so respected as a teacher, a man so sought after by the important musicians of his day, this priest so devoted to his task as to be made a canon of the Church, this composer who was to ascend to such a position in the history of French organ literature? The history of the family named Titelouze goes back to about the year of 1420. It was about this time that the first beginnings of this family came from England to France. This was the occasion during the Hundred Years War of the English domination of France which saw some marked migration of English families to the mainland. It was not, however, until about the year 1513 that the grandfather of Jehan arrived in France from England by way of the Netherland Republic under the domination of Spain. The archives of Saint Omer have a procuration dated 1513 approved for Katherine, widow of Guillaume Titelouze. About the year 1523 there are to be found several names of Titelouze. First is found the name Micquel Titelouze, grandfather of Jehan. This grandfather and his wife, Martine Maes had three children—two of which were sons, Lambert born in 1541 and Benoît whose date of birth is unknown. The third child was a daughter whose name is unavailable but who seems to have married a Marcq Le Precq. The older son, Lambert, married Jeanne Lanne. From this marriage a son was brought forth. This son, Nicolas, was born in 1562. About the year 1585 he married Antoinette Vasseur, and they had two sons, Pierre (1587 or 1588) and Loys (Louis). Nothing is found of the children of the daughter of Micquel after her marriage to Marcq Le Precq, nor can we locate the name of the woman to whom Benoît was married. It was from this latter marriage that Jehan Titelouze was born.

An Immigrant Family From England

It is interesting to investigate these relations to see just how these people happened to come to Saint Omer, and to learn something of their occupations.

Grandfather Micquel was a barber and had a shop within the shadow of the collegiate church at Saint Omer. Benoît was a fiddler, and we read also of Nicolas as being responsible for supplying music at banquets and festivals. Micquel evidently left England because of religious conflicts, and in doing so determined to associate himself with the family by the same name then living in Saint Omer. This early branch of the family had come to France during the Hundred Years War, as mentioned above. This was a fortunate choice for Micquel; for he spared himself some of the distresses of the more severe persecution under the rule of Elizabeth I. Saint Omer was a logical choice of location, since the Jesuits had established some schools to teach the refugees, as they were considered. Later a first college was founded at Saint Omer in 1566, while a second one was established in 1592. These were designed to assist in the education of the first group which departed from England under the first wave of persecution about 1560 and to coincide with the arrival of the second group escaping the repressions of 1587. This was the time of the youth of Titelouze, who was a contemporary of John Bull, Peter Phillips and John Dowland. The latter was attached to the English ambassador in France (1579-1588). It is also interesting to note the varieties of spellings of the name Titelouze. The name originated in England and was spelled Title-House. On the continent we find such other spellings as Tytelouse, Tithelouze, and Titelouse.

Of the name Titelouze, we find two mentioned during the life of Jehan. One, to whom is given the surname Louis, was a painter for the Collegiate Chapter and the other has no given surname. An interesting note concerning Nicholas is that he was in several references indicated to be the "German cousin" of Jehan the organist. Jehan, being a priest, was never married and thus had no heirs to claim the family name. So with this son of Benoît, the fiddler and supplier of social music for feasts and festivals, the musical name of Titelouze in any spelling disappears from all records.

Titelouze's Appearance in Rouen

Jehan arrived in Rouen from Saint Omer in 1585, when he was twenty-two years old. We are unable to find any reason for his leaving his native town, but in that same year he was appointed organist at the Church of Saint Jean in Rouen. It is possible that the political unrest could have effected a decision to come to Rouen, but Rouen itself was not spared association in the internal war which followed. It became a center of focus for the King, and Henry of Navaree came and laid seige to the city for two months before retiring unsuccessful. The city did capitulate two years later following the governor Villars-Brancas. At this time, Titelouze was thus at the organ of Notre Dame on the occasion of the enthroning of the young Cardinal of Bourbon, who at the age of twenty-eight followed his great-uncle, Charles IX of the Ligueurs.

Titelouze quickly made himself felt as an authority. He taught with a firm understanding of the theories of Zarlino (1517-1590) and Glaréan (Dodecachordon 1547). He was reputed to be an expert in interpretation, and he was well experienced in the art of organ building. These factors, coupled with the knowledge that the Chapter had hired him because as a priest he was an upright man and one against whom there was no charge of fault, made Titelouze a highly respected personage at the Cathedral. His devotion was such that the Chapter made him a canon in 1610. While waiting for his honor, he had to make application for citizenship or naturalization papers since there was a question of his not being French. In the year 1595 he made the necessary application for the papers, but the record of registration of these letters was not made until the year 1604.

The Organ of the Cathedral

In the year 1591, Titelouze resigned his position at the Church of Saint Jean. It would seem that the organ at the Cathedral required most of his attention, and his desire was to be faithful in one task as opposed to being only half attentive in two positions. The organ at Notre Dame, too, was more desirable. The Cathedral's instrument was one of great history. It was one of the first edifices in France to possess an organ, which possessed a choir to great or positif to great coupler. The instrument which Titelouze had here, however, was not so ancient as this. It was about one hundred years old and had been the gift of archbishop Robert de Croixmare. It was a rather sumptuous work, built for the French in their style by the German builder Oudin Hestre. The front pipes of this organ were part of the thirty-two-foot stop, and they were made of tin decorated in various ways. At this time, the organ needed to be rebuilt because of its age; and Titelouze persuaded the Chapter to engage Crespin Carlier, one of the truly great organ builders of the day, to restore the instrument to a state of more excellent service. This work was done in the years 1600 and 1601. In this rebuilding, Titelouze requested that the pedal board be extended to thirty notes, just two notes less than our present day American organs of standard design.

Organ Appraiser and Designer

This work all seems to have been done with the greatest of care and in perfect taste. Guillaume Costeley, the former organist of Charles IX, came to Rouen to inspect the instrument and pronounced that it was "in beautiful harmony". To tune this new instrument, Titelouze engaged Carlier, Valeran de Heman, and Guillaume Lesselier. These were three outstanding organ builders with whom Titelouze seems to have carried on very friendly relations. With such an instrument, one cannot help but realize the double source of interest in the visits paid Titelouze by his admirers and his musical contemporaries. He evidently was very much interested in building and design, since he was called to appraise a number of organs by various builders, including such as the organ of Notre Dame la Ronde built by Nicholas Barbier, the new organ restored by Carlier at Saint Jean in 1603, and the two organs built at the Cathedral of Poitiers in 1613. In 1623 he was called to the Cathedral at Amiens to inspect the new organ there; and some months before his death, he was called upon to draw up the specifications for a new organ to be built at the Church of Saint Godard in Rouen. This specification is of interest to see just how Titelouze calculated registration and stop requirements in his own thinking. This is a small, two manual organ, of course, but it does serve as a basis for consideration.

Grand Orgue:	Montre 16′	Fourniture avec reprises
	Bourdon 8′	d'octa ne en octave
	Prestant 4′	Cymbale III avec reprises
	Doublette 2′	de quarte en quinte
	Flûte 4′	Cornet V
	Petite Flûte 2′	Trompette 8′
	Sifflet 1′	Clairon 4′
	Quinte Flûte 3′	Regale pour servir de
	Petite quinte 1½′	voix humaine
	Tremblant, Rossignol et Tambour	

Positif:	Montre 8′
	Prestant 4′
	Doublette 2′
	Fourniture III avec reprises d'octave en octave
	Cymbale III reprises d'octave en octave
	Quinte flûte 3′
	Cromhorne 8′

Pedale: Bourdon 8′
Flûte 4′
Trompette 8′
Accouplement du Positif au Grand Orgue

His Interests Other Than the Organ

It was not only in the performance on the organ that Titelouze was interested. His compositions included not only the organ pieces but vocal music as well. He composed three masses—Missa quatour vocum ad imitationem, Messe à six voix, Missa votiva. The repertory of the choir at the Cathedral included these masses as well as works by Dufay, le Jeune, Bournonville, Guerrerro, du Caurroy and Lassus, to mention but a few of the composers represented. He was also interested in poetry and took part in poetry contests. He was made lauréat du Puy des Palinods in 1613 and again in 1630. The regulations of the Chapter did not permit Titelouze to take an active part in outside musical affairs; but in his later life, these rules were relaxed somewhat in view of his significant position in the realm of musical activity. Twice in 1631 Titelouze directed music festivals in honor of Saint Louis at the Chapel of the Jesuits. He was permitted much freedom in travel, and he did carry on a rather extensive correspondence. Some of this correspondence is still available for study, especially that which was carried on with Père Mersenne, with whom he enjoyed many hours of leisurely discussion upon the scientific and musical problems of the day. There was no one at Rouen with whom he could converse in such manner upon such then vital subjects; so, we see his journeys, especially to Paris where Mersenne was engaged, were of special satisfaction to him. It was evidently with much sorrow that he had to cancel his projected journey to Paris in 1633; for in May of that year he became confined to his room, and on October 25, six months later he died.

Organ Works

The organ works of Titelouze, which are composed of Hymns of the Church, to be played on the organ with fugues and variations on their plainchant and The Magnificat, or Canticle of the Virgin to be played on the organ in the eight modes of the Church, were published by Pierre Ballard of Paris. This first indicated volume was published in 1623 and the latter in 1626. It is necessary only to call to attention that the first volume of this work was the second such work for the organ ever to be published. The first was the collection composed by Frescobaldi and published in 1615. The following year after the appearance of the Hymns, Samuel Scheidt published his Tablatura Nova; thus this collection of Titelouze is very important from an historical standpoint. One can easily understand its unique expression of musical style as compared to those expressions found in the other two mentioned volumes. An investigation of these three works will show the strength of the French school at this time, and will aid in the conclusion that the continual developing mastery of French expression was equal to, and in some ways superior to, that of other musically leading countries. Let us here consider a few of the works to be found in this important volume and comment briefly upon some of the general characteristics of Titelouze's style as reflected in some specific examples from his works.

Discussion and Examples

This first volume of pieces composed upon the hymns of the Church was dedicated to Monseigneur Messire Nicholas de Verdun, counselor of the King. There are twelve hymns contained in the collection; and upon each there is composed a set of pieces, individually called versets. These hymns are as follows: Ad Coenam (four versets), Annue Christe (two versets and A-Men), A Solis Ortus (three versets), Ave Maris Stella (four versets), Conditor Alme Siderum (three versets), Exsultet Coelum (three versets), Iste Confessor (three versets), Pange Lingua (three versets), Sanctorum Meritis (three versets), Urbs Jerusalem (three versets), Ut Queant Laxis (three versets), and Veni Creator (four versets). The second volume published, that of the parts of the Magnificat, contains settings of these portions composed in the eight modes of the Church. These settings are very original and are possessed of the same dignity of style as evidenced in the versets of the hymns to be discussed presently. Of these eight arrangements , the one on the third tone seems to be the easiest in execution. No one complete setting seems to be any less valuable than another; however, there are some small degrees of worth expressed within each section in each section of the Magnificat.

The first hymn listed in the edition was the Ad Coenam. In the initial setting of this chant theme, the theme really occurs on the manuals. However, it is fortunate to be able to transfer it to the pedals, playing it on an eight-foot trompette. Here it will be heard above the ensemble on the manuals. Even if this is not done, the construction of the mixtures would provide for a positive sounding presentation, performed upon the manuals. Later editions of this work indicated that the

AD COENAM

Ad Coenam by Jehan Titelouze

p

(♮)
p
mf
(♮)
mf
(♮)

(♮)
Ped.
(♮)
(♮)
(♮)

UT QUEANT LAXIS

Ut Queant Laxis by Jehan Titelouze

manuals should employ stops of sixteen, eight, four and two-foot pitches with fournitures and cymbales added. The pedals indicated to have drawn the foundation and reed stops of the sixteen, eight and four-foot pitches. Recalling earlier remarks, this is not exactly what Titelouze would have considered to be an ideal registration. The second verset upon this hymn is in the form of a fugue in four parts. This is a solid and interesting piece of counterpoint. The composer here has created a rhythmically vital piece of music. The third verset is another fugue even more highly developed than the one found above. The fourth verset is a much longer work, and presents a fugue in four parts occurring over the theme itself which is stated on the reed stops in the pedals. This work becomes very much involved, and the motion is magnificent. It is a work of daring proportions written in a generally broad, expansive manner, very skillfully and seriously worked out.

The versets upon the Veni Creator are striking, but are better known musically from several editions. A somewhat more obscure work is that set of versets upon the Pange Lingua. This set of three versets is very much like those upon Ad Coenam, except that triple meter is introduced into the third verset, this occurring near the end of the piece. This triple meter returns to quadruple meter, and the work is finished in rapidly moving sixteenth notes.

Those versets upon the hymn Ut Queant Laxis are very interesting also. This is a very skillfully conceived set of pieces, and Titelouze's originality is foremost here. Of especial interest, one might call attention to the metric changes to be found in the third verset.

Conditor Alme Siderum is arranged to include three versets. The first of these is somewhat well known. It is a grave piece of writing in 3/2 meter. This work is often abused in performance, since some editions call again for thick sounds from the manuals and even thirty-two foot tone from the pedals. One should inspect this little masterpiece very carefully and choose a clear registration before considering a performance of the work. The second verset is composed of simple two-part accompanying material in the left hand, while the theme is stated on a solo stop or combination in the right hand. The third verset presents the theme developed in a four-part fugue setting which becomes especially complex near the end of the setting.

The settings of the Exsultet Coelum are grave, much as those of the Conditor Alme Siderum. The second verset has the theme presented in much the same manner as the Ad Coenam. The third verset is highly developed and longer, with strong harmonic implications derived from the contrapuntal texture found near the end of the piece.

The settings of the Iste Confessor are some of the most thoroughly developed

EXSULTET CŒLUM

Exsultet Coelum by Jehan Titelouze

mf
SENZA PED.
f
PED.

ff

pieces in the entire collection, while those upon Urbs Jerusalem are possessed of a very broad and dignified treatment, showing much contrapuntal strength.

From all these indications, it should be clear that the general characteristics of Titelouze's style include a seriousness of purpose, a dignity of treatment, a thoroughly developed musical presentation, a gravity of character, and a nobleness of concept. This coupled with the technique which the composer possessed, insured works of worthy intent and success born of sincere effort.

Titelouze's Own Words

It might prove profitable to include after this discussion, some portions of the introduction to the first volume Titelouze had published. Here we have in the composer's own words, some of the things which are reflected musically in his works.

"I could not bring myself to publish this little volume without the assurance my friends give me that it will be useful to those who desire to play the organ. It is this reason that has drawn it from me rather than the hope of receiving any praise from it, knowing well that among men there are captious souls who are more ready to reprove than to understand, who cannot see any work without trying to diminish its merit. And particularly when they can find a plausible pretext as it seems they can here, given that I practice, in a way perhaps new and unknown to them, not only some consonances, but also some dissonances. But not wanting to make myself a judge of this cause, and my subject not being at this time to treat of music in order to enlighten them about it, I refer them to those who really know the temperament which must be given to the tuning of organs, spinets, and other instruments, and why that is necessary; who know the augmentation and the alteration of major and minor tones, and other intervals, who understand the law of voices and instruments, they will learn from them that these tempered intervals can receive progressions and transitions that would not be given to voices; so that one can play on the organ a counterpoint which is better than one which is sung. So it is that I have held myself as much as I could to the general rules, by which I have recognized that Glaréan and others were right in saying that to understand music truly it is necessary that one play and know the order of instrumental strings; as indeed a great musician of our century has said to me countless times that he had sought this knowledge with affection, and it had been most useful to him, in this way putting his inventions into practice. The sieur du Caurroy and others have not neglected this study which has been a help to them in reaching the point at which they have arrived, and in recognizing that the instrument has something particular because of its temperament.

Now what has incited me even more to give this small work to the public has been to see volumes of tablatures of all kinds of instruments printed in our French; and it is beyond the recollection of men that any have been printed for the organ, the most accomplished instrument as to pneumatic genre as well to other genres, not only admirable in its construction, but estimable because of its use, thereby appearing that God has had His Church choose it to sing His praises. Besides the fact that we have increased its perfection in the last few years.

I have thus begun with those Hymns which are in the most general use in the various dioceses, in order to accommodate everyone, whose chants can be applied to several hymns according to the custom of the churches. I admit it would be desirable that in two or three of those hymns the modes or tones of the Church be better observed, as we shall do in free works, but the plainchant which has been accepted for so long in the Church being my subject constrains me to conform the fugues and counterpoint to it.

Now especially as the organ produces without difficulty all kinds of intervals, natural as well as accidental, I have used in some places some extraordinary ones (just and tolerable however) in order to give to this instrument that which is its competence, its own, and out of the ordinary; and I have even applied some sharps in places where I would omit them if it were for the voices, for reasons given above.

As the painter uses shadows in his pictures to make brightness and sunshine stand out, so we mix some dissonances among the consonances, as seconds, sevenths, and their answers in order to enhance their sweetness, and these dissonances make themselves heard as quite tolerable, well applied, and appropriate. The examples of good authors permit such.

Before concluding, I wish to warn the reader of three or four particulars. First, for playing two parts with each hand, I have used in some places the tenth, because there are a few organists who do not take it or should not take it. If there are any who have too small a hand, I have had affixed some reference marks to make it understood that one hand can help the other. These distances are used in order that the modulation of the lower and exterior parts may be better expressed, which parts one could not only extract, but also sing them because they have their themes distinguished and their pauses. For the length of the verses which treat the fugues, I could not make them any shorter, having three or four fugues repeated by all the parts on the subject. However, to accommodate oneself to the choir, one could finish at some period towards the middle, several of which I have marked to serve as an example. I also warn that there are some notes which have one point away from their character which I use only as a quarter of their value; it is to save a note and a tie which is necessary to signify it, also this point is in a place where it can have no further value. Adieu."

It would seem that the remarks contained herein above accent the earlier observations of the restrictions outlined in Part I.

MULTIPLE ASSOCIATIONS RELATIVE TO ANDRE RAISON

History Concerning Nanterre and Sainte Geneviève

Eight miles northwest of Notre Dame de Paris on the railroad to Saint Germain lies the small suburb of Nanterre. Here was the beginning of the musical life of André Raison as we know it. Nanterre is an old settlement in history. At the time of the Gauls, it was already a seat of Druid activity and possessed one of the temples of that ancient religious cult. The real significance for us, however, occurred about the year 429 A.D. when Saint Germain stopped at Nanterre and was impressed by the piety of a young maiden who lived there. She was much devoted to God and was zealous in His service. It is she who is pictured pleading with Attila to spare the village from his ravagings, and her plea seems to have been heeded. This occurrence was some time after her notice by Saint Germain. Geneviève, as she was called, was born in the year 420. She was nine years old, or thereabouts, when Saint Germain saw her. In the year 451 Attila crossed the Rhine, and Geneviève was probably past thirty-one years of age when she entered her plea with the leader of the Huns. Her works were of such note as to cause her to become the patron saint of Paris in later years.

Nanterre seems to disappear from the picture of history until the year 591. The importance of this occasion there was the baptism of the infant Clothaire II, son of Chilpéric and Frédégonde. In 1163 it is to be noted incidentally in a Bull of Pope Alexander III that Nanterre was in the possession of the Abbey of Sainte Geneviève. It has been reasoned that Clovis gave this territory to the abbey when he founded it on the south bank of the Seine. The village was ravaged by the English in 1436 and was subjected to all sorts of excesses and abuses.

Thanksgiving of Louis XIII

Much later in 1630, we note that King Louis XIII came to Nanterre to give thanks at the shrine of Sainte Geneviève for the healing of a malady which had stricken him while he was in Lyon. Also of note is the visit in 1636 by Anna of Austria, Spanish wife of Louis XIII. She came to the birth place of the saint to pray for release from the sterility which held her childless. Two years later her son, Louis XIV, was born. Several years later, in 1642, Anna founded a convent at Nanterre as a token of thanksgiving. The church there is by itself of no great interest. It was built during the thirteenth and fourteenth centuries and remained in that state of construction until about the eighteenth century. Nearby the church is the spring from which flow the miracle-waters to which people still make many pilgrimages. In 1657, to complement the construction of the convent, a seminary was founded at Nanterre. This also was under the patronage of Anna of Austria; and it was at this seminary that André Raison began his formal musical education.

Raison's Appearance

Sometime shortly after its founding, the seminary was enlarged in scope to offer a complete course in the humanities. As to the real value of the instruction received here, one might best determine this by noting that the University of Paris brought a lawsuit against the seminary, charging that it was an infringement upon its position as a University. After some time in court, the case was decided in favor of the seminary, which was allowed to continue in its projected functions. Thus, evidently the seminary was furnishing good instruction to an increasingly larger number of students in the continuing years.

We gain some information as to the work here from the introduction to the First Organ Book published by Raison during his lifetime. The book is dedicated to François Morin, Abbé of the Church of Sainte Geneviève of Paris and Superior General of the Chanoines Réguliers of the Congregation of France. Here in this introduction, Raison renders thanks for the years which he spent during his early life at the seminary at Nanterre where he seems later also to have taught. At the time of the publication of the organ book, he mentions that for twenty-two years he has served at Sainte Geneviève. Since we know nothing positive about his birth place or birth date, it seems nonetheless reasonable to conclude that since he evidently entered the seminary at an early age, that he was born either in Nanterre or nearby. The fact also that the rest of his life was spent in the abbey which owned the very ground upon which Nanterre existed, would seem to indicate a very close attachment to the place. Since there is such a close association between the abbey and the seminary, let us examine the situation at Sainte Geneviève itself to see into just what sort of a position Raison placed himself when he left the seminary to assume the duties of organist at the Abbey of Sainte Geneviève du Mont.

The Founding of the Abbey

The abbey itself was very old. It was founded by King Clovis (died 511) who established there the college of clerics. This was the religious body which later became known as the canons regular or the Chanoines Réguliers of which François Morin was Superior General at the time of Raison. The exact length of the observation of the regular life in the college is not definitely known, but we do know that in 1147 secular canons were officiating in the church. Pope Eugene III and King Louis VII, both aware of the disorders which prevailed, determined to make some reforms. Their first intention was to call in monks; however, the canons preferred some one of their own order, and in this matter the pope agreed. At the request of Suger and Saint Bernard, Gildwin, the first abbot of Saint Victor's consented to send Odo, the prior of his abbey. Saint Victor's was a logical choice, since a new canonical rule had recently been installed there. Odo encountered many difficulties in his noble attempts at reform, but his methods finally prevailed and some of the canons joined the reform.

Among the canons to join the reform was a young Canon William who was already well known for his learning and virtuous living. This man later had the duty of reforming a monastery of canons in the Isle of Eskil. Absalon, Bishop of Roskild, in Denmark, had known William when he himself had been a student at Sainte Geneviève. Knowing the canon personally, and knowing his virtues and abilities, Absalon had little problem in knowing the person to requisition for the needed reform. William was successful even in view of many obstacles and persecutions, and even managed to found another monastery which he dedicated to the Holy Paraclete. William died in 1206 and was canonized by Pope Honorius III. There existed for a long period of time close ties between the Abbey of Sainte Geneviève and its foundation in Denmark. Another young man named Peter, who had devoted his life to the abbey in Paris later became Bishop of Roskild; and Valdemar, brother of King Knut, died at the Abbey of Sainte Geneviève. This illustrious abbey, along with Saint Victor's and Notre Dame was one of the key forces in the founding of the University of Paris. Abelard even lectured here at the abbey school during his stays in Paris.

Reform at the Abbey

But, as was the general procedure of most religious houses which fell into the hands of abbots in commendum, relaxations of the regulations and other disorders were soon in evidence. About the beginning of the seventeenth century, Cardinal de la Rochefoucauld undertook to reform the abbey. From Senlis he brought a Holy Man by the name of Charles Fauré who previously had restored order to the very old abbey of Silvanect. He was successful in restoring the rule of Saint Augustine, and Sainte Geneviève became known as the mother-house of the Gallican congregation. After this reform, the history of the abbey was even more notable than before. By the middle of the seventeenth century the abbot-general of the congregation had under his jurisdiction more than one hundred abbeys and priories. The glory of the abbey continued unabated until 1790 when the revolutionary assembly declared all religious vows void and opened the doors of the monasteries. This was the end of this great and ancient monastery. Today this very building in which Raison worked in such an impressive historical surrounding is known as the Lycée Henri IV—a school for boys. Yet, in the works of Raison we can sense the impression of duty and serious mindedness which held sway in his surroundings then as he worked and composed for his fellow religious musicians.

The Tomb of Sainte Geneviève

It is most interesting when considering Raison to realize just how closely his life revolved about the ancient Sainte Geneviève, the virgin of Nanterre; for in his introduction he tells the Abbé François Morin that at the seminary he realized his purpose in life, and it was there that his formative years were spent. Then he was able to obtain the position in the abbey which controlled Nanterre. Just across from the abbey is the famous Panthéon which stands on the highest ground on the left bank of the Seine. This is the site of the tomb of Sainte Geneviève. Originally there was a small chapel erected over her tomb, but this was succeeded by a church which Louis XV vowed to build when he was ill at Metz in 1744. It was this chapel which Raison could see and visit when he wished. The present building was erected from 1764-1790 from designs by J. G. Soufflot and was dedicated to Sainte Geneviève. One year after its completion it was converted into a Panthéon or temple of fame for the burial of famous men. Mirabeau was the first to be buried there on April 4, 1791; and later, on July 12, the remains of Voltaire were brought there. It was restored to divine service in 1806, but was again made a Panthéon after the July Revolution of 1830. Even again it was reopened as a church in 1851, but it was finally secularized for the obsequies of Victor Hugo. Possibly the only thing which remains of the Sacred which originally was dedicated to the saint is the little chapel in Nanterre and the spring of water which is reported to have some healing power.

What of André Raison?

With these details of background, let us now examine the man Raison to see just what can be established concerning his history, personality and work. There is no known record of his birth or any mention of his death. A little inspection of relative dates might show something of his approximate birth date, however. According to the preface in his first published organ book, he had been at Sainte Geneviève for twenty-two years. The last piece in the volume, an Offerte upon "Vive le Roy", was written to celebrate the entrance of the King Louis XIV into the Hôtel de Ville on January 30, 1687. Since the book was published the following year of 1688, by mere subtraction we could see that Raison came to the abbey not later than the year 1666. Consider also that he studied at Nanterre and then taught at the seminary, we would have to grant that he was at least twenty years old at the time of coming to the abbey, and probably twenty-five years of age. This would put his approximate birth date in the first case during the year 1646, and in the second, the year 1641, which would seem to be the more logical date. We do know from the writing of his known student, the illustrious Nicholas Clérambault, that Raison was at the abbey still in the year 1720. We know also, from Raison's own remarks in the Second Organ Book of 1714, that he was organist at the church of the Jacobins in the Rue Saint Jacques. In this position he was succeeded by Clérambault by the year 1720. This is gained from the preface to the fourth book of cantatas published by Clérambault in that year, in which he gave himself the title of organist at the Church of the Jacobins. This could mean either that Raison was then dead by the year 1720 or that he had resigned that one position in favor of his esteemed student and remained as organist at the abbey until some later date which is impossible to determine. From all these various writings, it would be taken to indicate that Raison was then still alive in 1720 and still organist at Sainte Geneviève. We do know that Antoine Dornel had a rather long stay at the abbey after Raison left there. If we assume that Raison's death occurred the following year of 1721, this would make Dornel twenty-six years of age when he assumed his duties there. This is a very reasonable age, and would seem to be about that which is ascribed to Raison when he was employed at the abbey. Dornel died in 1765.

With the assumed date of birth of 1641, then Raison would have lived to about eighty years of age. This would seem rather old, but when we examine the lengths of lives of several of his contemporaries, we find that one of them, Guillaume-Gabriel Nivers, lived to the age of ninety-seven years; and another Nicholas Gigault, lived to be eighty-two years old. Henry du Mont lived to seventy-four and le Bègue was seventy-two, while Marchand lived to be sixty-three in spite of his peculiar type of living.

More Obscurity

At first it seems strange that a man who held such a position as Raison held should be so little known. He was not even considered in the writings of his contemporaries, and so we have great difficulty in finding anything positive about him or his life. Much of what can be discovered has to be reached by inspection of his works and a study of a particular personality in a peculiar geographical situation which certainly contributed to his obscurity. We read nothing of him in the writings of two of his near contemporaries. Titon de Tillet in 1732 published his Parnasse Français in which he mentioned the famous musicians of the times. He gave praise to several men by name, including Charles Piroye. Yet, Charles Bouvet, writing in Revue de Musicologie, the November issue of the year 1928, provided us with an article entitled Charles Piroye: un musician oublié—indeed a forgotten musician. However, the works of Raison were much available at that time, while one would scarcely have heard of Piroye, much less of having available his works. Writing about the same time as Tillet, d'Aquin in his *Literary Histories of the Century of Louis XV* mentions nothing of Raison, while giving due credit to the works of Clérambault.

It is rather to turn to the writings of Clérambault himself that we find the tribute which befits the genius of Raison. In his dedication to Raison of the Organ Book published in 1710, he stated that he should confess that if the works he was to present therein had any merit, it was due to the patience, teaching and encouragement he received from his most respected master. It is not necessary to quote in toto the remarks of the grateful student; they are obviously somewhat overdone in statement. But the fact is that Clérambault, a musical genius in his own right, had the power of discernment which enabled him to realize that he had had the advantage of studying with a great musician and an excellent teacher who was sincerely devoted to the task which confronted him.

"Vive le Roy"

Returning to this point of obscurity, one of the factors which contributed to Raison's lack of recognition is that he evidently never played at court, and was consequently not known by the associations there. Even if his name had been mentioned and somewhat known, the fact remains that few of the people connected with the court or musicians of other churches who appeared there had ever seen him or met him personally. His "Vive le Roy" was written to be played at the return of the King and was not conceived as a work which he himself would appear to perform. This work, which is belittled by some and merely indicated by others to have been conceived in the tastes of the times, is really a fine work. One cannot really agree with M. Norbert Dufourcq in the suggestion that Raison has to be pardoned for his attempts to imitate the cries of the people reaching Heavenward in thanksgiving for the return of the health of the King. Descriptive music had been written many years before this, and no apology is due on that basis. As to the lightness of the divertissements, we are thankful. When one considers the boldness of the introduction, the power and majesty of the harmonic structure, the dissonances and effective embellishments, the lighter movements are welcome as a logical consequence to such an introduction, and make a fitting relief for the jubilant conclusion of full organ. Here the theme is projected with all the power of embellishment by the majesty of the powerful reed stops and draws to a fitting conclusion a work of some length and grandiose proportions.

Raison's Devotion to Duty

Another factor to consider in this obscurity is the very nature of Raison's development from childhood. He seems always to have been a retiring person, one who lived at the seminary and worked there without any particular thought of the outside world. In his dedication he is thankful again for the years there wherein he was able to discover as it were the very reason for his existence. This reason seems to have been the great desire for service which permeated his whole being. This would seem to have been best done in the seclusion of the monastery walls so far as the musical work of the man was concerned. Here was his organ, his students, the many services he had to play and the opportunity to compose for the edification of the Catholic services.

This great devotion to duty and purpose can be read even further in his own writing. In the instructive introduction to his musical publication he shows a real concern for the persons who are to play his music, directing his remarks to the cloistered brethren who did not know how musical things were accomplished in the churches of the cities. His detailed registrations and general comments concerning registration and the moods of the various types of pieces and how they were to be performed all show that he was concerned about his fellow musicians who were confined to the services of the Church. This shows real humility of purpose, an effort to supply something which is needed and not with the thought of making a name for André Raison.

It was not a question of writing some trivial ditties for some untrained monks; for he comments that if two or three organists be available, they can divide the playing of the Masses among themselves so that the more proficient could perform the more difficult movements. He also adds that the person who supplies the easist movements would by no means have the least interesting music to play; for he has tried diligently to provide within the scope of easeful execution music which is at the same time valuable and noteworthy. In addition to this attempt at real service, he indicates that some pages have been left whereon the organist can write the chants that are peculiar to his own service. He also offers to compose music for any specific chant if so desired, provided that the reader will send him a legible copy of the chant he wants set to music. All this seems to indicate rather clearly that we are concerned with a retiring man who is dedicated to the task which he has set for himself—that of service to his Church and Her servants without much thought of himself. Again, his dedication expressed real humility and is concerned wholly with this element of finding service in his work. This retiring character, then, is another factor in the mystery, as it seems to be, which envelops Raison.

Where He Lived

Still another feature in all this obscurity was his living habits once he had located himself in Paris. As indicated before he seems to have come directly from the seminary to the abbey. When he first arrived in Paris he took up quarters in the Rue Saint Etienne des Grez in the house of the Guardian Angel. This was on the property of the parish of Saint Etienne du Mont. The house was so named because of the fact that outside a window on the second floor was a placque which contained the figure of an angel. This window seems to have been from a room which was used for sick persons. This was a modest dwelling having no more than two stories to the structure. It was while living in this house that Raison published his First Organ Book. Here he was very close to the abbey and had only about the modern equivalent of two city blocks to walk to his work.

After 1687 he moved to more elegant quarters at the intersection of the Rue Saint Etienne des Grez and of the Cholets. This house was called the Sacrifice of Abraham. It was a much more desirable location, so far as accommodating features were concerned. One would feel that after twenty-two years of faithful service Raison should be allowed a little more luxury in living. This house had two large stories on top of which was an entresol or half story on top of which were three more stories and an attic. At the rear was a storage room, and between the back of the house and an outside storage building was a courtyard. Under the whole of the house was to be found a sizeable cellar. Of course, Raison merely had a room in this building and did not have access to the whole structure. Here he was near to his work also. The distance seems to have been about the same, except in another direction.

Raison's name is not mentioned anywhere in the civil enumerations of Paris. This would seem to indicate that he had lived on church property all his life there. Since the church properties were free from taxes, the occupants did not have their names entered in rent listings. This is another element in the utter seclusion of the man. Here he lived and worked for two churches all within an area that today would not exceed four city blocks. Evidently his organ was a fine one at Sainte Geneviève, judging from the correspondence with M. Clicquot. This would be a factor in keeping him near his chosen task as well as the fact that there were mostly likely innumerable services to be played each week. One cannot help but recall the fact that when Couperin le Grand went to Saint Gervais, the total number of services for which music was to be provided was estimated at three hundred fifty to four hundred during the year.

Raison Responds to Clicquot

In a letter to Raison, Clicquot asked that Raison send to the Monsigneurs at Notre Dame de Rouen some information concerning the tonal qualities of the positif of his organ and the distance from the montre to the positif. Raison indicated that he was happy to comply with Clicquot's wishes and would be glad to receive any visitors who might want to hear the organ for themselves; further that he would be agreeable to entertain them and to see that any information wanted was supplied. This would seem to indicate that Raison was agreeable enough to have people come to see him if there was something he could do to help them. However, he must have been very backward about visiting other people. When we consider the nearness of the Abbey of Sainte Geneviève du Mont to some of the other important churches of Paris, this becomes increasingly clear to us.

Retirement

Most of the reason for this man's obscurity is with the man himself, as would now seem to be clear. He had but a short distance to go to visit his colleague Buterne, a famous student of du Mont and organist at the Church of Saint Etienne du Mont. During his stay at the abbey the illustrious Louis Marchand had for a time the position of organist at the Church of the Jesuits in the Rue Saint Jacques. It might have been a piece of good fortune for us, in historical perspective, if he had met and made the acquaintance of this man who later became the organist at Saint Benoît, at Saint Honoré, at the Chapelle Royale and at the Cordeliers. Raison could have met Marin de la Guerre, organist at the Sainte Chapelle and husband of Elisabeth Jacquet, clavecinist and composer whose compositions received the attention of the King himself. He could have traveled the short distance at some time during his stay at the abbey to the Church of Saint Nicholas du Chardonnet to have met Jean-Nicholas Geoffrey. The aged Nivers was at Saint Sulpice, at not too great a distance from the abbey. He might possibly have had the opportunity of meeting de Grigny when the latter was organist for a few years at Saint Denys; or perhaps he could have made the effort to cross the river to visit the famous François Couperin le Grand, organist at Saint Gervais.

But all this Raison evidently did not do, and as a possible result we are held in such utter absence of the real facts of his life itself. From all that we can read and determine in his music, however, it would seem to be a life much as has been indicated thus far—a life of consecration and dedication, one of selfless living, one of extreme devotion to duty as it was made clear to him, one content to work and live to work, to sacrifice without the thought of sacrifice, to labor only with the joy evident, a life of retreat within the established confines of the Church. So then lived André Raison, a man with a reason—one which he determined and by which he lived and served.

His Music

With these thoughts about the musician, let us look briefly at his music and specifically at a few of the movements from his masses to determine some of the musical characteristics of this composer. If we consider all the pieces in the masses and the Offerte upon "Vive le Roy" which compose the First Organ Book, we can draw the following conclusions about the general style of Raison. Here is a composer who is certainly no poet. We have here no one of the strength of de Grigny. There is little of the very expressive in his works. There are very few works of the form of Récits, few expansive passages for solo stops, and few works of great tension such as are found again in de Grigny. Here is a man of much method, one who is very proficient at counterpoint, and one who is careful in his presentations. However, even in view of this technique, his inspiration is not always of the first order. Within this limitation, we find that his forms are also limited to a certain extent; and within this further limitation is a somewhat noticeable repetition of material and idea.

On the other hand, we find a musician and composer of great strength in harmonic movement—a composer who can project a certain majesty of purpose even in his limitation. Raison's contrapuntal inventiveness is probably the greatest of his day. He could take his place only slightly below Titelouze in this area of music. We find that his embellishments fall generally into three types —the mordent, the inverted mordent and the trill in longer form. Twice in the Offerte does he use the coulé and never is it used in the movements of the masses. His use of embellishment borders somewhat on the profuse, but it is less in evidence than in the works of le Bègue, for instance. Yet we might note in passing that a rather extreme case exists in the Offerte. There are two hundred forty-five embellishments in this one work. Also peculiar to Raison and occurring in the works of no other composer of this period of French organ music examined is the curious use of the pattern of a sixteenth note followed by a dotted eighth note. Both these notes seem always to be of the same pitch.

Considering the movements for individual investigation, we should note the first Kyrie of the first mass. It contains three of the prominent features of Raison's style. In it we note the use of rolled chords, rather profuse ornamentation and the peculiar dotted pattern mentioned above. Also of note in the harmonic character of the piece is an oscillation between flats and naturals and sharps and naturals, creating a type of fluid inexpectation. Herein are contained flourishes of sixteenth notes with thirty-second notes introduced on the weaker parts of divided beats. These thirty-second notes are fingered by Raison in such a way as to suggest that these were probably played in detached fashion. Each of the notes is marked to be played with the third finger, hence non-legato.

In the second setting of the first Kyrie we find a piece of considerable intensity. The pedal part is performed on the eight-foot and four-foot reed stops while a four-part contrapuntal texture is executed on the manuals. This not an easy work, since there are many embellishments, a long trill in the pedals and continuous four-part writing in sustained style to be performed by the hands. The two concluding measures are in the form of a highly colorful cadence. Counterpoint in general is strong and imitation is used to a great extent. The final Kyrie is quite a charming piece in triple meter.

MESSE DU PREMIER TON

(KYRIE.)

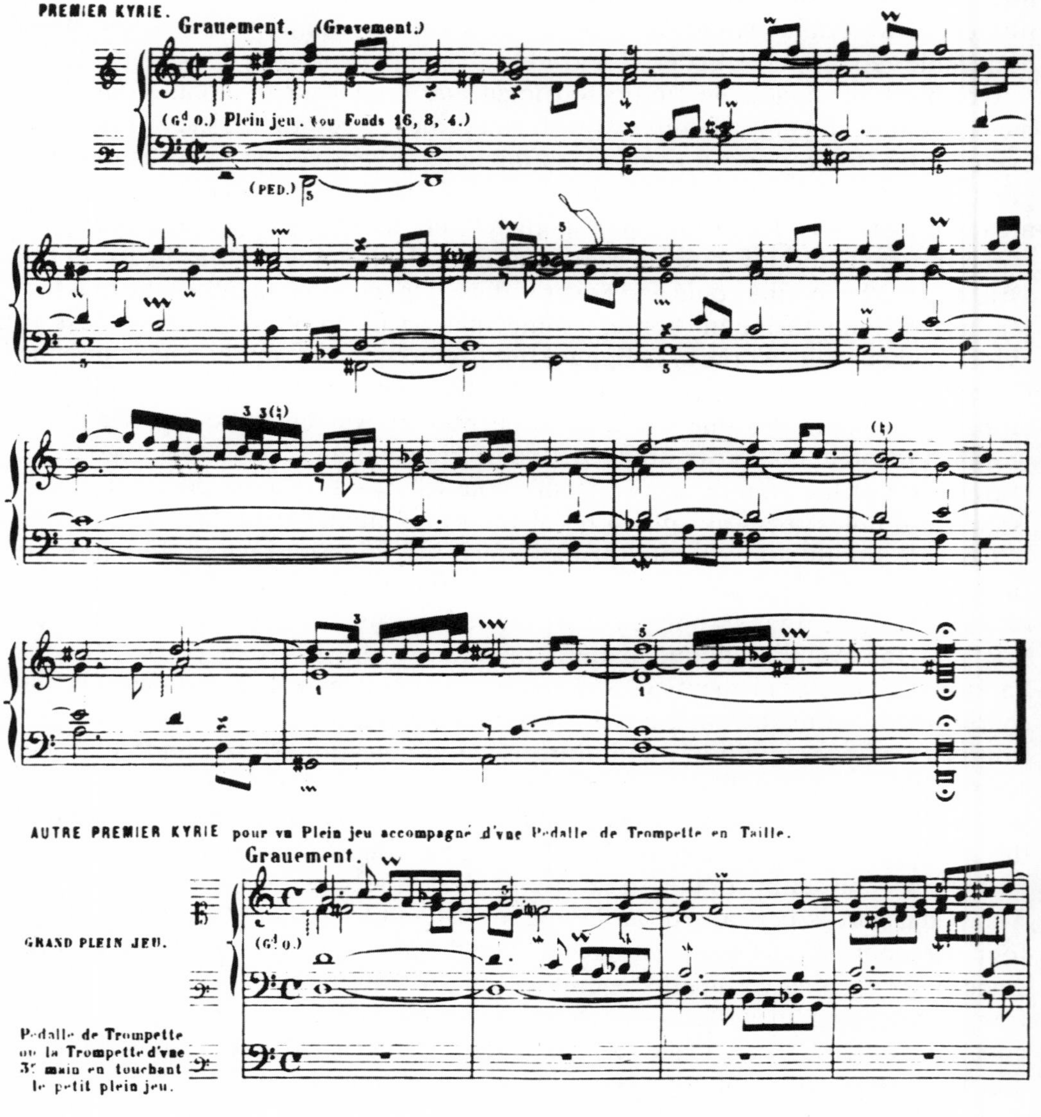

PREMIER KYRIE.

Grauement. (Gravement.)

(Gd O.) Plein jeu. (ou Fonds 16, 8, 4.)

(PED.)

AUTRE PREMIER KYRIE pour vn Plein jeu accompagné d'vne Pedalle de Trompette en Taille.

Messe du Premier Ton (Kyrie) and (Sanctus) by André Raison

L'jntention de l'Auteur est de jouër aussi le plein jeu sans la Pedalle.
Dans l'édition originale cette pièce est notée ainsi. (ALEX: G.)
Autre premier Kyrie pour vn plein jeu accompagné d'vne Pedalle de Trompette en Taille.
Grand plein jeu grauement.
Pedalle de Trompette ou la Tromp. d'vne 3e main en touchant le petit plein jeu.
Grand plein jeu grauement
(etc)
(A. G. 97.)

AMEN DIALOGUE.

(*) C'est à dire la main droite sur le Gd. O, la main gauche sur le Positif, et vice versa.

(SANCTUS.)

SANCTUS.

The Et in terra pax of the Gloria shows strong use of imitation and the use of the characteristic rhythmic pattern. Herein also are found the familiar rolled chord techniques. The Domine is a very expressive piece of writing, but still existing within the confines of the contrapuntal concept. The Qui tollis is an odd work with scalar flourishes skipping back and forth among the cromorne, cornet and some echo stops. The fact that this type of writing occurs here, and calls for the use of the great organ would lead us to believe that the organ Raison had at the abbey was one of four manuals. The A-Men of the Gloria is a vigorous work which is interrupted near the end by two and one-half measures of slow, expressive material but which concludes with the vigor and freshness of the earlier parts. The Elévation is an interesting trio in triple meter for manuals and pedals. Here again counterpoint and imitation are much in evidence. The Agnus Dei (first setting) is the most expressive piece in the mass. Its elevated character is interrupted once with an allegro section which is strongly reminiscent of the last Kyrie.

The second mass has many of the features of the first. One should note the famous Christe movement in the form of a passacaglia and especially the fourth Kyrie. This work has as its theme one which is reflected strongly in a later work (Dialogue and Musette) by Jean François d'Andrieu. The Benedictus is an interesting piece of closely knit imitative writing.

In the third mass, the second Kyrie is in the form of a fugue and is a rather interesting movement. The last Kyrie is a more extended and embellished work. The Qui Tollis should also be mentioned as a work worthy of much consideration. The Benedictus is in trio form and again is a piece of very thoughtful and thorough imitation. The Elévation is a very sustained and impressive work which is interrupted by seven measures of gayly conceived material in triple meter. The Agnus Dei is a beautiful work of alternately fast and slow passages. It should be noted that in the edition of Guilmant, that four sharps are obviously misplaced in the second and third measures.

In the fourth mass one could note the second Kyrie as an expressive piece written in imitative fashion. This piece is longer than usual and is of very somber character. The Christe is a beautiful Trio en Chaconne which is rather well known from Raugel's edition. The last Kyrie is a lively work of some length. It consists mainly of alternating sections on the grand jeu and petit jeu. The second Sanctus is a stilted Récit de Tierce, a type of composition Raison seldom had occasion to write. The Benedictus is a moving work, strongly polyphonic in conception. As in the other masses, the Elévation here is a piece of great beauty and expression.

(AGNUS.)

(1) RECIT, Fonds et Anches, boîte ouverte.
Gd O. Fonds de 16, 8, 4. Récit et Pos. accouplés au Gd O.
POS. Fonds de 8 et 4.
PÉDALE. Fonds de 16 et 8. Tirasse du Gd O.

(A. G. 97)

Agnus Dei by André Raison

(1) Même observation qu'à la page 16.

The fifth mass is composed on the eighth tone and opens with a Kyrie composed in a broad style in five parts. This work calls for reeds in the pedals. After seven measures of introduction in tense four-part writing, the pedals enter with moving eighth notes under a four-part structure of half notes. The fourth Kyrie is a lively work of marked rhythmic character, strong and bold and full of inventiveness. The Domine of the Gloria is a trio in the form of a gigue. Strong, dotted rhythmic patterns are accented by effective embellishment to make this a truly delightful piece. Probably the most expressive of the pieces is the one which concludes the fifth mass—the Deo Gratias. This is a work of poetical beauty unlike any such writing that Raison has given us heretofore in the masses. In the form of a Récit de Tierce en Taille, it is a fitting conclusion to the masses. It is a quiet, meditative thanksgiving, so typical of the true spirit of André Raison.

Deuxième Kyrie by André Raison

Petit jeu.
(RECIT.)
Grand jeu.
(Gd O.)

DEO GRATIAS ou autre piece.

Deo Gratias by André Raison

(*) RÉCIT, Bourdon de 8, Basson de 8, et Clairon de 4, boite fermée
POS. Bourdon ou Flûte de 8, Flûte douce de 4
PÉD. Bourdons de 16 et 8.

(A. G. 97.)

FIN DES MESSES

(A. G. 97.)

ARAISON

NICHOLAS DE GRIGNY – MASTER AT RHEIMS

Music in earlier days was an art and an enjoyment which was to a large extent cultivated within a family circle. One reads a multitude of histories of families who developed very considerably in the practice and performance of musical arts. Likewise, one is many times made aware of the greater number of lesser, insignificant and inconsequential families and individual personages who struggled in the shadows of the art either in pleasant diversion or in the search for a meager livelihood.

The Family and Their Occupations

At this time there occurred in the famous city of Rheims the family name of de Grigny or Desgrigny, as it was at one time written. From whence came this family at its origin we are altogether unable to determine, but in 1626 the name of Robert de Grigny is noted in the rent listings in Rheims. He was at that time renting a house which belonged to one Nicholas Colbert and in the civil notation he is indicated to be a qualified performer and teacher of instruments. While this mention is rather late, it would seem to indicate that as one of a family the name and training would date well backward into the sixteenth century.

There were many occasions which called for musical services, affairs of both frivolous and serious nature. Many festivals were held in the towns, and there were numerous assemblies of various sorts. It is noted that on August 18, 1653, one Jean Gouge became affiliated with Regnault Pasté, Thomas Mortet, Robert Joret, Robert Mortet and Robert Leclerc. The duties of these men were concerned with the organization, rehearsal and performance of suitable music at all assemblies of the town.

A number of the de Grignys were hired by other musical persons to perform musical services. Louis Constantin engaged Jean de Grigny in 1642 to perform and be his assistant in the city and at country and rural affairs. This Jean was a performer on the stringed instruments and was one of considerable achievement. This is to be learned also from the fact that the title of "king of the violins" was given to Louis Constantin.

As was the nature of many of this type of musician, these de Grignys were not very secure, financially speaking. This family had attached itself to music as a means of making a livelihood and nowhere until 1671 do we find anyone of serious musical worth. In such a situation they many times found it difficult to meet all the financial obligations which befell them. We read with interest the various burdens which had to be borne from time to time. Some of the family who were organists owed debts to their blowers and were continually in disagreement over the payment of such debts. One member was sued by a baker for debts incurred in receiving bread. Still another account tells of a member's having been billed consistently by a butcher for chickens bought before a New Year's Day as a gift for a father-in-law. Yet another owed the wool-comber and launderer for combing and bleaching some wool and for repairs made to his clothes at the laundry. It is also noteworthy that such events are not confined either to the de Grigny family or to the century in which the members lived.

As mentioned, some of these people were organists. Two which can be named for certain are another Robert de Grigny who, in 1665, was in the services of the church of Saint-Symphorien; and still a different Robert de Grigny who, in 1675, was the organist at Saint-Hilaire. Another member, Louis de Grigny, Nicholas' father, served the Cathedral of Notre Dame of Rheims upon the death of his son in 1703. It was this son Nicholas who stands forth in the history of this French family. Louis, the father, was also engaged in another form of musical activity at the same time. As a performer on other instruments, he was much in demand at weddings and at the numerous festivals and assemblies of the town.

The name of the family is found often, but as to the domestic history of any of its members we are ignorant. It is known by various civil enumerations that the de Grignys had various interests from 1656-1663. Some, in addition to playing for assemblies and festivals and other civic affairs, attached themselves to bands of entertainers and evidently made sufficient monies to live more comfortably. These bands of performers were widely engaged to play for parties and other domestic festivities. Finances would seem to have improved for we find no more records of lawsuits or other litigations. So to this father, Louis, and his wife Elizabeth, née Debauve, was born Nicholas de Grigny in the city of Rheims.

Let us recall something of the history of this famous city to see into just what sort of situation this Nicholas was born. It was an ancient city. It had been the old capital of the Remi, the least warlike of the Gallic tribes whom Caesar had fought and had admired. In a new era of Roman occupation it assumed another important role after 200 A.D. when it again became a capital—this time of a notable division of the Roman Empire, Belgium Secundum. During this period it became a center of culture and of active education. It has been compared to Athens at that time as a center of cultural activity.

During this same period, that of the third century, two churchmen of great future importance journeyed to Rheims. Saint Sixtus and Saint Sinicius were the men and in the upper part of the city they established their see. This represents the beginnings of the ecclesiastical organization in the city. Rheims was ravaged by the Vandals and later by the Huns under Attila; however, this did not diminish its importance. From the time of the conquest by the Franks the history of Rheims has been closely associated with the history of the Church. A brief consideration of a few of her clergymen will show some of the important historical events connected with the church.

It was Saint Remegius, born about 440, who, December 24, 496, baptized Clovis, the king of the Franks. It was also he who effected the marriage union between Clovis and Saint Clothilda. Saint Remegius laid here the foundation of the political authority and the religious power of the See of Rheims which was to manifest itself in later years. From this time forth Rheims was a power of reckoning in the church and commanded much respect in Rome. Sometime later we could note the name of Bishop Hervé (900-922). It was he who spent much effort and had great influence in the labor toward the conversion of the Normans. Also one should note Archbishop Adelbero (969-988) as he labored in the name of the church in the political entanglements which saw the rise of the Capetians to the throne of France. The political endeavors of Archbishop Arnould (988-991) and (995-1021) as a partisan of the Carlovingian house and the forceful occupancy by Gerbert (991-995), who later became archbishop of Ravenna and still later Pope Sylvester II, are also indications of the prominent role of Rheims.

It was a bull of Sylvester II issued in 999 which recognized the right of the archbishop of Rheims to crown the king of France. In 1359 the English king, Edward III, marched upon Rheims with the intention of being crowned the king of France. He was repulsed successfully; however, in 1420 Henry V succeeded in capturing the city. Nine years later saw a most famous historical reversal. It was in 1429 that Charles VII drove out the English and was, in that glorious moment for France, crowned king under the standard of Joan of Arc.

Here Cardinal Charles de Lorraine founded the university in 1547, and its English college became a focal point for English Catholic endeavors in the reign of James I and Elizabeth I. Further importance can be inferred from the facts that Rheims has given to the Catholic world five popes, twenty-three archbishops, fifty-three cardinals and a very considerable number of bishops.

Birth and Childhood of Nicholas

Into all this color and influence of history came Nicholas de Grigny. It has been stated that the date of his birth is impossible to determine. It is listed in various places as 1671 or 1672. It has been pointed out that the state archives of Rheims do not yield a baptism record for him. That is easily understood. It has been indicated that in the register of Saint-Etienne there is to be found a reference to the date of February 14, 1671. This indicates the baptism of a de Grigny child who, it has been argued, was Nicholas, his name having been inadvertently omitted from the record. This author has a copy of that entry from the parish register of Saint-Etienne. It clearly states "14 fevrier 1671—Bapteme de ANDRE, fils de Louys de Grigny et d'Elizabeth de Bove". According to the copy of another document (Nicolas de Grigny, organiste de Notre-Dame de Reims et sa famille, par P. Gosset, Secrétaire Général de l'Académie de Reims) the date of September 8, 1672 is given as the date of baptism of Nicholas de Grigny. This baptism occurred in the church of Sainte-Pierre-le-Vieil, the parish of his godfather and of his godmother. According to the custom of early baptism, the child could have been but a few days old on September 8, 1672. The total of positive facts about de Grigny's short life is exceedingly small. Nicholas, as a boy, developed in the shadow of the Cathedral of Rheims. He was a member of the choir, which at that time was under the direction of Jean Caillet (1662-1680), of Jean Talon (1680-1684) and of Jacques Rousseau, Talon's successor. Talon was dismissed by the chapter because of his negligence and poor treatment of the boys. Here in the choir de Grigny was exposed to the influence of serious music and, with the exception of Talon alone, serious-minded musicians. François Cosset (1647-1662) and Jean Caillet had done much to preserve the more serious style of the ancient masters from the influences of the styles of such men as Auxcousteaux, Métru and Gantex which were then prevalent.

de Grigny in Paris

After some study with the local musicians of Rheims, de Grigny journeyed to Paris to focus his training and to endeavor to become the serious-minded musician we know him to have been. Here, through the earlier acquaintance in Rheims of Estienne Enocq, the famous organ builder, he met Nicholas le Bègue (1630-1702). From le Bègue, de Grigny was able to have some important lessons which later affected his style. Also through the acquaintance of Pascal Collasse (1649-1709) he was able to meet the musicians of the court and the theatres. Collasse, who reached his height as a musician of influence about 1680, was one of the four masters of the chapel of the king. Through Collasse, de Grigny was also able to make the acquaintance of Henry Lesclop, another important builder of organs.

Here in these surroundings de Grigny was able to learn many different things and to develop without too much influence from any one person. From le Bègue he could derive aid in stylistic composition in religious music; from the court and theatre musicians he could gain charm from their useful techniques, and not of the least importance was an understanding of the very effective use of organ registers to be acquired from the aforementioned organ builders. It was here in Paris also in 1693 that he obtained a position as organist at the Abbey of Saint-Denys, possibly through the influence of le Bègue. De Grigny remained at Saint-Denys until 1695.

Nicholas's Marriage and Family

Most sources say that de Grigny served the Cathedral of Rheims from 1695 to 1703. However, in 1695 he is listed in a Paris directory as a musician of the highest standing in that city. In that same year he married Marie Magdeleine de France, a daughter of Nicholas de France, an established merchant in Paris. The occasion of the journey of the de Grignys to Rheims the following year, 1696, was to have their infant daughter, Marie Anne, presented for baptism at Saint-Michel on May 11 of that year. On May 25, 1697, a son, Louis, was presented for baptism in the same church. A second son, Nicholas Charles, was baptized July 4, 1698. The record of this baptism contains the first mention of the fact that Nicholas de Grigny was employed as an organist in Rheims. Here he is listed definitely as the organist of Notre Dame of Rheims. It would appear that he was probably employed at the cathedral sometime between May 25, 1697, and July 4, 1698. In 1700 another child, Anne Geneviève, was baptized at Saint-Michel and in 1701 still another, Jean Françoise, was presented. Concerning these children we know nothing and after the death of Nicholas, the only fact mentionable is that his father, Louis, followed him at the organ of the cathedral. These meager, yet interesting details are all that can seem to be found concerning this serious musician. However, beyond the mere factual and historical elements of existence, there is something to be learned about the man himself. In the expressions through his compositions can be found several features of personality which stand out in bold relief, telling of the musical character of the man. To discover a few of these identifying features it is well to consider a few of his organ works.

The Livre d'Orgue

The complete collection of his works appears as a set of forty-nine pieces in a volume called simply Livre d'Orgue. This little volume contains a mass, five hymns and a Point d'Orgue. This collection appears in several places. In 1904 Durand and Company published an edition by Guilmant based upon an edition by Christopher Ballard published in 1711. This early edition is to be found in the National Library in Paris as Volume 1834. However, the Royal Library of London possesses a copy of pieces by de Grigny entitled First Book for the Organ containing the mass and other pieces bearing the date of 1700. Jean Pierre Theodore Nehrlich owned this copy in 1788. It has been reasonably well established that this copy was made from an earlier copy made by J. S. Bach in his own hand about 1703, judging from the character of the writing of that time. When this book was published after de Grigny's death it was merely given the title of Book for the Organ.

In general analysis what are some of the features which characterize the writings of this neglected man? There is a great continuity of form in all his writings. There is no hesitation in the flow of the musical lines; he conceives no sharp angles, but concentrates upon a smooth flow of motion in even the smallest details. There is to be found a symmetry of development in all his works. The listener is led carefully through the mazes of musical complexities with reason and clarity. His works abound in color, not in the artless use of profuse ornamentation, but through written-out, delicate musical embellishment. When ornamentation is used it has evolved as an integral part of the musical thought and does not have to become a part of the music upon repeated hearing. There is a certain character of robustness and heroism in some of the themes, especially in the dialogues. Here also can be found a dynamic rhythmic vitality instead of the use of oddly dotted patterns for effect. In more contemplative works there can be found a truly profound sentiment. Undoubtedly inspired as well by the awesome sculptured decorations, the beautiful glass windows and the colorful tapestries of the cathedral itself, de Grigny manifests a truly religious character in his musical thought. One has but to hear his Récit de Tierce en Taille in a proper setting to realize that a man of profound religious conviction was its composer. Of additional significance are the elegance and refinement of style so in evidence even in the least extensive compositions. And, finally, in the general science or concept of musical writing de Grigny surpasses his contemporary countrymen. A certain inevitability appears in his music as it is heard. Every note, each phrase, all fit into a preconceived whole which seemingly could not have occurred in any other way. Here is to be found the sure test of a composer and de Grigny emerges as a master.

The Music Itself

It is not difficult to locate these characteristics in the works themselves. In the first setting in the mass, the Premiere Kyrie en Taille, can be found a boldness expressed by continuing dissonance. Four-part counterpoint occurs around the theme, the counterpoint being imitative and colorfully embellished. The theme occurs in whole notes within this structure, composed predominantly of eight notes. Herein can be noted a symmetry of development and a continuity of form.

The Fugue on the same kyrie subject, the second piece in the mass, is a very sustained work. It is highly expressive, considerably ornamented and dissonant. The falling sixteenth-note figures produce an elevated effect. The conclusion is syncopated and ornamented. The piece is well worked out and is proof of de Grigny's artistry in the techniques of composition. Attention to proper registration is of paramount importance. It is composed in such a way as to have two voices sounding on the cornet and two on the cromorne with a fifth voice occurring in the pedals on a stop of four-foot length.

The third piece, Cromorne en Taille à Deux Parties, is an example of the composer's ability to conceive a piece of rare suspension. The right hand performs two voices played on eight-foot foundation stops, while the left hand executes two parts on the cromorne stop, the pedals playing a fifth part. The two solo parts are in imitation as are the other two upper parts. This is a beautiful work of great intensity and contemplation. It is filled with emotional restraint and decorated with profuse and vital ornamentation.

1.er Kyrie en Taille, à 5 (*)

Première Kyrie en Taille, á 5 by Nicholas de Grigny

(*) Claviers: Tous les Fonds et le Plein-jeu.
Pédale: Fonds et Anches de 8 et 4 P.

(**) Noté ainsi dans l'édition originale:

The sixth composition in the mass, Et in Terra Pax, is a lyrical and flowing setting in 6/4 meter. This is an excellent example of the interesting treatment which can be constructed within the bounds of a simple, non-harmonic plainsong theme. Although the work is but a little more than one page in length, it is a true masterpiece in miniature. Herein dissonances are treated boldly and embellishment is effective. The conclusion is one of rather daring harmonic consequences for the period in which it was written. The theme occurs on a solo stop of probably four-foot length and the four-part contrapuntal texture surrounds the theme.

Cromorne en Taille à 2 Parties by Nicholas de Grigny

Herein is a highly successful solution to the problem of providing a worthwhile work which involves setting up a consonant harmonic pattern upon each long note of the chant. This, coupled with the fact that only one note of the theme occurs per measure and further that one does occur at the beginning of each measure, offers a real problem to the composer.

The three settings of the hymn Pange Lingua are indeed representative of the deep religious thought evidenced throughout de Grigny's works. In the first verse the theme occurs in the tenor supported by three other voices. Notable in this setting is the rhythmic interest and intensity of the writing itself. The theme is composed of a five-note falling figure suggestive of the great Fugue in five parts found in the mass. This piece of three pages is beautifully constructed in imitative fashion. Although an expansive work in conception, it is coherent and musically symmetrical. The setting of the second verse is in the form of a fugue in five voices. This too is a broadly conceived work of considerable length for a French fugue of this period. The piece is highly embellished and is filled with tension, created by much dissonant movement. De Grigny's mastery of structure is in evidence in the strength of the texture of this work. It is colorful and highly developed musically. The third verse is a Récit du Chant. This work is well known compared to most of the others listed thus far, since it is readily available in present-day anthologies. The chant theme enters after seven measures of introductory material. The whole work is typical of that element of loftiness which pervades the composer's contemplative pieces. The intensity of the theme in its embellished form could only have been conceived by a master composer.

In the Offertoire sur les Grands Jeux, found in the mass, one finds a work of somewhat considerable length. The piece is planned in two distinct sections and a third concluding section. The first division is in a 4/4 metric pattern. This section begins in a fugal fashion only to develop later into a setting of a solo-type theme heard against a contrapuntal background. There is some alternation in registration as some quasi-echo passages are introduced. The second section appears in a 6/4 metric pattern. A rather lengthy fugal introduction develops into a statement and reply pattern with manual alternations occurring one measure apart. A seventeen-measure stretto over a pedal point concludes the large work. Here again continuity of form is obvious. There is a certain heroic character in the themes which are further marked by vigorous presentation.

Mere mention of the famous Fugue in five voices from the mass will be sufficient here. It occurs in contemporary anthologies and is surely well known. A simple five-note scalar figure is expanded into a most profound and highly elevated composition. Its only surpassing work, the Récit de Tierce en Taille, is without doubt one of the most intense compositions ever composed for the organ. The title means, of course, a recitation or theme in the tenor part played upon the jeu de tierce. This is a very provocative piece of ornamental writing. It is truly a profound expression of elevated thought. Much linear motion is achieved in this work by profuse ornamentation. The theme appears everywhere either in exact form or in suggested imitation. Upon first hearing or playing, the work seems to be a through-composed piece; but upon close inspection, one finds that de Grigny's genius for design has given this impression in a work which contains continual repetitions in part or in whole of almost everything with which it begins. It is a work of vast poetical beauty and somber reflectiveness. The ornateness of the theme is perhaps suggestive of the ornate sculpture work in the cathedral and the intense atmosphere of the whole piece is one in which we can sense the ceiling of heaven in a world all the musician's own.

To know the man Nicholas de Grigny one must perform his works. To do this one needs patience, historical perspective and understanding of the musical flexibility necessary for the expressive manner of ornamental execution. With these qualities in evidence in performance, de Grigny, from an obscure, remote, provincial organist, becomes a dynamic musical personality.

Récit de Tierce en taille(*)

Récit de Tierce en Taille by Nicholas de Grigny

(*) Positif: Jeux doux de 8.
Récit: Cor de nuit, Gambe de 8 et Octavin doux de 2.
Pédale: Jeux doux de 16 et 8.

(**) Cet accord est écrit ainsi dans l'édition originale:

(***) Ecrit ainsi dans l'édition originale:

(*) Ces huit notes sont en triples croches dans l'édition originale.

(*) Une double croche et deux triples croches dans l'édition originale.

SAINT QUENTIN AND ITS ORGANIST PIERRE DU MAGE

Historical Items About Saint Quentin

Two canals join three rivers at Saint Quentin. The Somme is connected with the Scheldt by the Saint Quentin canal and with the Oise by the Crozat canal. On the right bank of the Somme at this junction stands the ancient settlement now known as Saint Quentin. During the era of early Roman military conquests in this area, the town was centered around the meeting place of five military roads. It has been plagued by armies and wars and their companion, destruction, since that time. The Romans called this place Augusta Veromanduorum. It was the ancient capital of the Gaulish Veromanduens. The name of Saint Quentin came later, and commemorates the famous Latin missionary, Gaius Quintinus. He was successful in establishing a firm beginning of Christianity in the district around Amiens. In the year 287 A.D. he, along with two Christian companions, Victorious and Gentianus, was put to death at the present day site of Saint Quentin upon the order of the Roman prefect Rictius Varus.

It is impossible to determine the exact date of the establishment of the bishopric here; but we do know from church records that about 532, Saint Quentin was transferred to the ecclesiastical dominion of Noyon. Because of the influence of Noyon's bishops upon the development of Saint Quentin, let us comment briefly upon one or two items pertaining to this location. Noyon was called Noviodunam Veromanduorum by the Romans. It was noted as the residence of the great bishops Saint Medard and Saint Eloi. Here in 768 Charlemagne was crowned King of the Franks. The half-Gothic and half-Romanesque towers of the Cathedral of Notre Dame de Noyon have been acclaimed by architects as one of

Collegiate Church of Saint-Quentin: reeds of the Great Organ.

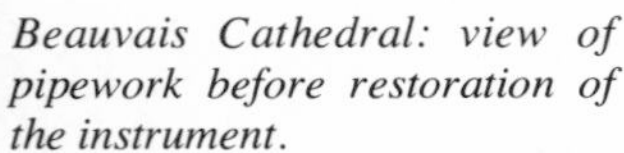

Beauvais Cathedral: view of pipework before restoration of the instrument.

Collegiate Church of Saint-Quentin: view of the new pipework of the organ rebuilt by Haerpfer of Boulay.

the finest specimens of the period of transition in France. The older of the cathedral buildings was burned in 1131. The present structure was begun shortly after the destruction of the original cathedral. Upon viewing it seems difficult to believe that much of the present building antedates the year 1150. It is known that the transepts and crossing date from about the year 1170. The nave seems to have been constructed beginning about 1180, while the west front and towers are of the early part of the thirteenth century. In Paris at Notre Dame, one sees examples of experimentation in architecture, a certain searching element which is noticeably absent in the positive atmosphere created by the certainty and assurance found in the structure here at Noyon. Here is a stern deliberateness which is a reflection, as it were, of the necessity of certainty.

In 1293, the whole of the town of Noyon was consumed by fire, and the glorious cathedral was wrecked. However, with the same touch of deliberateness, it was again rebuilt, this time with the sexpartite replaced by quadripartite vaulting and a finishing of the magnificent buttressing. This is still a famous cathedral and church seat, and it was through the efforts of Saint Eloi, Bishop of Noyon, that the collegiate chapter was established at the tomb of Saint Quentin. This establishment was effected about the middle of the seventh century, at the time Dagobert was King of France. As a result, this tomb became a famous place for pilgrimages.

In 883, the town was surrounded by walls; and under Pippin, grandson of Charlemagne, it became one of the principal strongholds of the counts of Vermandois. In 1080, Saint Quentin received from Count Herbert IV a charter, one which, in 1103, was further extended. The town was occupied by the Burgundians from 1420 to 1471, and in 1557 it was captured by the Spaniards. During the engagement, Philip II made a vow to construct the Escurial if he might be successful in the battle there. This building, located about twenty-seven miles north of Madrid, was a result of this vow. The Spaniards held Saint Quentin for two years, but it was returned to France in 1559. In 1560 it was bestowed as a dowry upon Mary Stuart. This meant that until her death, she was to receive the revenues of the town.

The Church Itself

One of the remarkable buildings in Saint Quentin is the famous Hôtel de Ville, and near this unusual structure is to be found the Collegiate Church of Saint Quentin. This is considered by some authorities to be a marvelous example of Gothic architecture of the twelfth, thirteenth and fourteenth centuries. There is some authoritative agreement that this church was planned by Wilars de Honecort. The vault, dating from the thirteenth century, is one hundred and twenty-seven feet high. It has two transepts, probably the only such example remaining in France. An additional effect of height has been given by the vaulting shafts which rise from the floor. There is a single aisle to the nave; but the choir, dated 1257, had two aisles divided by cylindrical columns. The chevet has chapels ranging with the outer aisle and opening by triple arches to the ambulatory.

The size of this church is almost sufficient to make it a cathedral. The earliest part of the church is the western tower which seems originally to have been detached, standing as a campanile. As early as 1113 a reconstruction of the church was begun, but it is not certain that this building was ever completed. The choir of the present structure was erected in the early thirteenth century. Saint Quentin has been plagued by cracking masonry. Just after the choir had been completed, cracks began to appear, and the buttresses and flying buttresses had to be strengthened, and longitudinal tie-rods were inserted. In 1316 more cracks appeared; in 1394 the high vaults of the choir had to be repaired. From 1468 to 1474 the choir again had to be restored and tie-rods were inserted across the central aisle. This was not enough to stabilize the building completely; but it still stands, and since the fifteenth century no serious efforts have had to be taken because of natural reasons. With its double transepts, a polygonal chevet, double side aisles and complete set of radiating chapels, it offers a remarkably interesting plan of construction.

Under the choir and dating from the eleventh century is a crypt containing the tombs of Saint Quentin and Victorious and Gentianus. The Church of Saint Quentin is in that area of France which contains a veritable multitude of splendid old churches and cathedrals, each a marvel of some phase of architecture. It stands about forty miles southeast of Amiens, about twenty-four miles south of Cambrai, and thirty-two miles north-northwest of Laon.

The Organ is Dedicated

On March 15, 1701, in this famous town made so important in the Middle Ages because of its cloth manufacturing, there was dedicated at the Collegiate Church a beautiful organ built by Clicquot and Vedeau, master carpenter of the buildings of the King. It is interesting to read the comments of the organist there at the time—Pierre du Mage—addressed to the Venerable Doyon Canons at the Chapter of the Royal Church of Saint Quentin. ". . . the construction of your organ which is without doubt one of the greatest, the most sumptuous, and the most perfect instruments in the whole world, . . . ''. The organ had been rebuilt as new by the father of the famous organ builder, François Henri Clicquot (1728-1791). In 1736 this organ seems to have been repaired by Thierry, eminent organ builder of Paris.

Who Was Pierre du Mage?

But who was this Pierre du Mage, the organist who had expressed such lavish praise for the organ? He was a student of the illustrious Louis Marchand, where or when we do not know. His dates of birth and death are likewise unknown. He is somewhat like Raison, in that what is known of him is told entirely by him in his own writing. This material is contained in the dedication page to his Livre d'Orgue and on the cover page. As one studies the music, the evidence of some of the truly glorious aspects of his teacher Marchand are quite apparent. However, as one looks further, more than this is obvious; for here are expressions wholly original, projections of a future music, as it were.

It might be good to call attention to Fétis and his comments about du Mage in his famous ''Biographie Universelle Des Musiciens'' (deuxième édition, Librarie de Firmin Didot Frères, Fils et Cie., Paris, 1863). He states that ''deMage'' was organist at Saint Quentin about 1752 and was a pupil of Marchand. He composed a book of pieces which was published in 1753. Now in 1752, du Mage was no longer at the training school at Saint Quentin. This is gained in part from some church records which indicate that at a function on August 29, 1746 the church organist named Monceau was heard in performance. The organ pieces were not published in 1753 but in 1708. However, du Mage was, as Fétis stated, a student of Marchand.

The organ book entitled ''First Book for the Organ'' contains a suite in the first tone and is ''dedicated to the gentlemen, the Venerable Doyon Canons and the Chapter of the Royal Church of Saint Quentin''. This volume was printed by Roussel of ''la rue de la Pacheminerie du côte de la rue de la Harpe''. It was to be sold by du Mage at Saint Quentin, by Roussel at his shop in Paris and by Richard, builder of clavecins in the Rue du Paon, also of Paris.

du Mage's Own Words

One does not know the duration of du Mage's stay at Saint Quentin. Records are lost or do not give this information, and we are unable to determine the exact relationship between this organist and the chapter. In reading the dedication, one seems to sense that it is a trifle overdone in humility and respect. Whether this was the true nature of du Mage, or whether he was trying to secure himself in his position, we cannot know. The fact that he promised another volume and did not produce it could mean several things. Either the first was not very well received and a second not encouraged or he was not at Saint Quentin after 1708 to accomplish this projected task. Possibly the pieces were written and used by him, did not find their way into print and were subsequently lost. At any rate the total of the musical and literary output of Pierre du Mage as we can know it is contained in these eight pieces which comprise the organ book and the cover page and dedication found therein. The dedication reads as follows: "Gentlemen: the honor I have to be your organist, the daily expressions of good will which I receive from your company, prompt me to dedicate to you this first of my musical works which I have composed and have tried to write according to the technically skillful school and in the taste of the illustrious Mr. Marchand, my teacher. I do not dare to flatter myself that they are worthy of the great zeal that you have for the divine service or that they could in any way answer to the magnificence that you have made apparent in the construction of your organ which is without doubt one of the greatest, the most sumptuous, and the most perfect instruments in the world; but I hope at least that if the audience get some benefit from this first suite of organ pieces and from the other ones that I will compose in the near future in each key, that this audience will be incited to share and to augment the gratitude that I owe you, and that you will be so good as not to decline this mark of respectful subservience with which I have the honor to be, gentlemen, your very humble, very obedient and very obliging servant—du Mage."

The Composer

As we study this man as a composer, we are impressed by a real element of power and grandeur. The suggestion of power is somewhat like that found in Raison, a real boldness and forthrightness in harmonic movement. The grandeur is reflective of some of de Grigny in the scope of design. Du Mage then, is a master of the harmonic consequences of polyphonic writings. In his works dissonances are more skillfully used than in those works of his predecessors, except de Grigny. Du Mage is capable of writing long sustained passages of successive dissonances; and in this man we recognize a combination of poet and a man of logical order. These eight pieces show much variety in writing yet show a style which is always even and consistent. Here is probably the last of a great line of French organ composers beginning with du Caurroy and Titelouze. After du

Mage, there is no organ composer of equal merit until the advent of César Franck.

A study of the last one-fourth of the Trio found in the Organ Book will reveal a strong relation to the harmonic feeling of some of the Crucifixus of the Mass in B Minor of J. S. Bach. Other passages found in the Duo and the Basse de Trompette are strongly suggestive of some of Beethoven's writings. The importance of the volume of pieces cannot be too strongly indicated. As with the book of de Grigny, Bach also had a copy of this one by du Mage, and it was known to his students as well. In further examination of the organ book we note a tenderness and expansive writing of the highest order in the Récit and in the Tierce en Taille. A majestic architecture is evident in the Plein jeu; beautiful harmonic realization is striking in the Trio; the fugue is important because of its structure and skillfully achieved polyphony. In the Basse de Trompette one is aware of much reason and design, in the Duo, precision and worth; and a tremendous unification of broad, expansive dissonant writing, effective use of echo and splendid fugal writing with selective embellishment throughout are distinguishing features of the concluding Grand jeu.

Personality Reconstructed

One knows nothing, of course, of the real personality of du Mage; but if, as is the case with most composers, he has indicated to us something of his individual nature in this set of pieces, we could draw these conclusions as some which seem to impress as one hears the music and studies it. Here would seem to be a man of several moods—a sincere and honest workman with a training, a vision, an ability and a purpose probably out of proportion to the situation and especially the musical tastes of his particular time in French history. It is conceivable that here we are confronted by a serious musician of uncompromising character in an era when organists had succumbed to the continual searching for mere tonal effects and had entered upon the facile descent of mere virtuosity and parasitic ornamentation.

Du Mage was evidently endowed with that rare combination of logic on the one hand and of uninhibited expansive expression usually found in persons possessed more of mood and less of firm and ordered reason on the other. It is possible, as has been mentioned earlier, that more pieces as promised were not forthcoming because of the lack of acceptance of this volume by the purchasing public. A comparison of this volume with certain others would provide some strength to this argument. It is true that Christopher Ballard published in 1711 the significant volume by Nicholas de Grigny; but, having died in 1703, de Grigny did not live to offer a second volume or to determine the general acceptance or rejection of his only book. Clérambault, publishing in 1710, does not present material quite of this caliber; and furthermore, his reputation was not alone as an organist or composer for the organ. Because of his conflicting lofty intentions in a situation tending toward more trivial tastes, it is reasonable to believe that du Mage was not long at Saint Quentin after 1708.

The Music

Let us examine this Livre d'Orgue of du Mage and see the individual characteristics of the pieces.

Plein jeu: this work is in two distinct parts or sections. The beginning of the first part consists primarily of scalar type flourishes in the right hand, with a left hand complementary part beginning with the third measure. Measures seven and nine have left hand flourishes under sustained chords in the right hand. These are not the customary pure scale passages found in many works by other composers, but are only of scalar type. Imagination is foremost, and the concept of musical breadth which is discovered again and again in du Mage is immediately in evidence. There is a moderate amount of embellishment in this first section, but it is such as to be highly effective and not merely a matter of form. The cadence which concludes this section is composed of some successive seventh chords. This introductory portion is executed on the positif. At its conclusion a sustained and majestic section of continuous four-part writing occurs. This portion is indicated to be performed rather slowly as compared to the allegretto introduction. Dissonances are nobly presented, and the harmonic movement is very strong. Embellishment is less than moderate. Inversions of chords and seventh chords are used with a great feeling of interest. The movement is smooth and flowing. This section is in an almost chorale-type style. It is beautifully and skillfully worked out. Unlike many other contemporary works, this one possesses a sense of breadth and much power.

Fugue: This work is unlike other pieces with this title by French composers. One here is reminded of the fugues by Roberday. The theme is presented logically by successive entrances, proper breakdown, some development and a conclusion with stretto. Entrances are in order from soprano to bass. The rhythmic pattern consists of a dotted quarter followed by an eighth note. This pattern is stated four times followed by six notes in descending order. The second and third quarters are embellished. Ornamentation is again judicious. Seventh chords are frequently encountered, and the linear motion is admirably constructed. Rhythmic interest is inherent in the nature of the theme itself, but du Mage does not let it become a tiresome repetition. In the breakdown he writes a section of smoothly flowing counterpoint which attracts more interest in its vertical consequences than in the linear motion achieved. This is then destroyed by a two part section which ushers in the theme itself. The piece is not exactly an easy one in execution. The work shows skill in contrapuntal technique and a clear concept of concise construction. The final three measures broaden to half-notes and provide a very positive conclusion.

Fugue from Livre d'Orgue by Pierre du Mage

Trio: This work is composed in three parts, two parts being in the right hand and one part in the left hand. A three measure subject is introduced in the uppermost part and is followed a fifth below by the entrance of the second part. Four measures later the lowest part enters. The independence of the upper part breaks down for a few measures as parallel thirds are introduced in eighth notes and some parallel sixths appear in quarter notes. After eleven measures of this, the upper parts again show independent movement, and imitation and sequential treatment are prominent. The theme is presented thoroughly in all parts and developed extensively. There is no extraneous material presented. Everything that occurs appears immediately and is used in various manners throughout the work. We see again not only obvious skill in the technique of countrapuntal inventiveness, but also real originality and the ability to compose a fine work in small form. Ornamentation is moderate and renders this work somewhat difficult in accurate execution. The careful interweaving of the moving parts produces an interesting work of much merit. The Trio is best performed upon contrasting combinations of stops rather than upon solo type stops.

TRIO.(*)

Trio from Livre d'Orgue by Pierre du Mage

* Positif ou Récit: Flûtes de 8 et 4. Nasard 2 2/3 *ad libitum*.
Gd Orgue: Gambe et Bourdon de 8.

Tierce en Taille: This expansive work is one of great beauty of expression. Here we find a somewhat different kind of solo from those in vogue in du Mage's time. The theme begins as an arabesque type subject, but just past the middle of the piece, it broadens for the most part into slow-moving quarter notes. Five measures from the end, the arabesque motif is suggested, as the work concludes in quiet manner. Two and three-fourth measures of three-part writing for soft stops begin the work. The solo enters in quarter notes with reserved embellishment. It proceeds quietly and with much flexibility. The upper parts as executed by the right hand are very sustained and contain notes of long value. After nine measures of more reserved writing which follow the florid introduction, one measure of sweeping motion generated by notes of small value is heard. This is followed by a solo passage composed of notes of longer value resulting in a more deliberate type of motion. Dissonances in this broad section are such as to increase the natural tension in this type of work. Flexibility in execution is of paramount importance, and a properly chosen tempo is needed to reflect the intentions of this colorful composition.

Basse de Trompette: This work is in the form of variations upon a short theme presented as a solo by the middle of the three parts forming the composition. The theme is three measures in length and is almost wholly of quarter notes. At the end of the third measure, the uppermost voice enters in imitation of the theme. Four measures later the theme is heard as a solo on the trumpet or trompette stop, this time occurring in the lowest part as the title suggests. After five measures of quarter notes, of which over thirty percent are embellished, the theme is expanded

Tierce en Taillé from Livre d'Orgue by Pierre du Mage

(sic.)

into three measures of sequential nature, composed in eighth notes. Throughout the execution on the trumpet stop, the accompaniment is composed primarily of half notes and whole notes. The theme is begun again with some variations. After four measures of quarter notes, two measures of eighth notes are encountered, followed by two measures of quarter notes then two more measures of eighth notes, concluding with a two-measure cadence. A five measure interlude, suggestive of the theme is followed by another variation with some rhythmic alteration. The presentation is expanded to about three times the original length of the theme. At the conclusion of this section, there occurs a one measure rest in the lowest part. Here again the theme is begun and is expanded to such proportions as to represent one-third of the total length of the composition. The piece employs a wide range of the trumpet stop, thus adding interest to the color. Unlike some works in this form, this piece is not based upon an attractive rhythmic pattern, but is designed as a smooth, flowing piece. The Basse de Trompette is impressive in its expanding thematic material and provides a piece of much interest. The imagination of du Mage is obvious here and again his harmonic strength is well represented.

Récit: This piece is a very charming work of expressive beauty. While basically in three parts, chords are built up occasionally at critical points in the motion of the composition. The theme is one of a high degree of embellishment and represents some very intense musical construction. There are four types of ornaments used—the mordent, inverted mordent, turn and grace-type note. This is a through-composed piece, having no repetition of thematic material, no imitation between the parts and no sequential passages. The work is artfully designed to avoid these devices, and yet the entire piece is of complete contrapuntal design. The Récit falls into several tense climaxes with ensuing passages of repose. The spacing of the points of climax is well designed so that one is not conscious of any undulating motion of obvious nature as the work unfolds. Dotted notes are used very effectively and tied notes are used to heighten the rhythmic tension. Some of the ornamentation is written out note for note instead of being symbolically indicated. Four measures of dramatic flourishes conclude this imaginative piece of melodic writing. Inventive genius, one of the key factors in the power and strength of the writings of du Mage, marks this piece as a real masterpiece of musical expression.

Duo: The theme of this work is two measures in length. Embellishment here is slight. The motion obtained in this writing is mainly contrary or oblique and does not consist of incessant repetitions of passages in thirds, sixths or tenths. The theme is often expanded to three measures. The piece sounds much like a theme and variation composition. The last one-fourth becomes a great expansion of the original two-measure motif. In the sequences which occur here, one is reminded of later works of the Classical Era. This is a truly interesting composition, showing some very skillful techniques in two-part writing. It is lively, rhythmically strong and fluent in impression.

Grand jeu: This energetic composition opens with a sweeping scale-passage, culminating in a tonic chord. The whole first part of the three distinct divisions into which the work is cast, is one of chordal character with a dialogue-type figure with four thirty-second notes occurring first in the pedals and then on the manuals. A short subdivision featuring the solo leap of a fourth upward followed by two chords is then heard. The upper note of the leap is always embellished, and the upper note of the second chord is also ornamented. The subdivision is of sequential character and is repeated. The first statement occurs on the primary ensemble and contains pedal notes. The second part of this subdivision is somewhat like an echo and features a smaller ensemble and no pedal part. After nineteen measures of this majestic and vigorous introduction, a fugal section occurs. Voice parts enter successively; and after sixteen measures of this style of writing, a measure of full chords ushers in a development of the material on a subsidiary manual. Before the entrance of the pedals, both hands are again transferred to the primary ensemble. A brief echo section ensues; and after seven measures of the original material, a slower, rhythmical, embellished third section on full organ concludes the composition in a broad, sustained style. This work shows great originality, strength of musical character, an understanding of effective embellishment, and a clarity of style and development. In this concluding work in the Livre d'Orgue, du Mage leaves us a really fine composition of uncompromising character. It would be difficult if not impossible to find an organ composition written in France after the date of this volume which could measure up to the qualities found in this work. It remained for Franck to equal and perhaps surpass this great effort.

Grand Jeu from Livre d'Orgue by Pierre du Mage

(PED.)
(♮)
Positif.
(S.PED.)
(G^d O.)
Recit au dessus.
(POS.)
(♮)
Grand jeu.
(G^d O.)
(PED.)
Positif.
(S.PED.)
Grand jeu.
(G^d O.)
(PED.)
Positif.
(S.PED.)

Echo.
(RÉCIT fermé.)
Grand jeu.
(G!O.)
Positif.
Echo.
(RÉCIT.)
Grand jeu.
(G!O.)
(PED.)
(S.PED.)
(PED.)
Gravement.
(ff)
(S.PED.)
(PED.)

Bibliography

Bible of Saint Etienne Harding, A.D. 1109 Ms. de Citeaux, Bible de Dijon, Nos. 12-15. Municipal Library, Dijon.

Manuscript—Latin 7295—Bibliothèque Nationale, Paris.

Le Roman de Fauvel (Gervais de Bus) Ms. F. Fr 146. Bibliothèque Nationale, édité en phototypie par Pierre Aubry, Paris, 1907. La musique es dans le 1er vol. de Polyphonic Music of the XIV th Century avec un vol. de commentaires par Leo Schrade. Oiseau-Lyre, 1956.

Res. Vm7674; Vm 1852; Vm 674. Bibliothèque Nationale, Paris.

V. 461; Ms. 2372; Ms. 2365. Bibliothèque Ste. Geneviève, Paris.

New Catholic Encyclopaedia. McGraw, Hill Book Co. New York, New York. 1967.

Fétis, F. J. Biographie Universelle Des Musiciens (Deuxième Edition), Librairie de Firmin Didot Frères, Fils et Cie., Paris 1863 Culture et Civilisation. 115, Avenue Gabriel Lebon, Bruxelles, 1963.

Holweck, Rt. Rev. F. G. A Biographical Dictionary of the Saints With an Introduction on Hagiology. St. Louis-London. 1924.

Attwater, Donald. A Dictionary of Saints—being also an Index to the revised edition of Alban Butler's "Lives of the Saints". London, 1938.

Jadart, M. H. Les Portraits historiques du musée de Reims 1er fascicule, 1888. P. 53 à 86.

Pirro, André. Histoire de la musique de la fin du XIVe siècle à la fin du XVIe. Librairie Renouard, Paris, 1940.

Bedbrook, G. S. Keyboard Music From the Middle Ages to the Beginning of the Baroque. MacMillan and Co. Ltd., London, 1949.

Agnel, Arnaud. Les comptes du Roi René III. Piccard, Paris, 1910. (pp. 240-241).

Goodrich, Wallace. The Organ in France. The Boston Music Company, Boston, 1917. (p. 114)

Dufourcq, Norbert. Musique d'Orgue Française de Jehan Titelouze à Jehan Alain. Librairie Floury, Paris, 1949.

Dufourcq, Norbert. Le Livre de L'Orgue Français. (1589-1789) Editions A. et J. Picard, Rue Bonaparte 82, 75 Paris, 1971.

Citron, Pierre. Couperin. Series "Solfèges". Editions du Seuil. Rue Jacob 27, 75 Paris. 1956.

Dufourcq, Norbert. Jean Sebastian Bach. Librairie Floury, Paris. 1948. Pp. 138-185.

Rokseth, Yvonne. Archives Nationale LL 112, p. 52 in Musique d'Orgue. E. Droz, Paris, 1930. P. 356.

Raugel, Félix. Les Grands Orgues des Eglises de Paris et du Department de la Seine. Librarie Fischbacker, 33 Rue de Seine, 33 Paris.

Aubrion, Jean. Journal de Jean Aubrion. Edited by Larchey. Metz, 1857. (p. 275).

de Tillet, Titon. Parnasse Français, J. B. Coignard Fils, Paris, 1732.

Cram, Ralph Adams. The Heart of Europe. Charles Scribner, New York. 1915. The Gothic Quest. Revised edition. Garden City, New York. Doubleday, Page and Co. 1915. My Life in Architecture. Kraus Reprint Co. New York. 1969. The Ministry of Art. Houghton Mifflin Co. New York and Boston. 1914.

Adams, Henry. Mont-Saint-Michel and Chartres. Houghton Mifflin Co. New York and Boston, 1913. Republished with a new introduction by Lewis Mumford. Collier Books, division of The Crowell-Collier Publishing Company, 1963.

Mersenne, Marin. Harmonie Universelle. Translated by Roger E. Chapman. Martinus Nijhoff, The Hague. 1957.

Beaucamp, Henri. L'évolution de la musique d'orgue française depuis la fin du XVIe siècle jusqu'à nos jours. Travaux de l'Académie des Sciences, Belles Lettres et Arts de Rouen pendant l'année 1932. Rouen, 1933. P. 148.

Williams, C. F. Abdy. The Story of Organ Music. Charles Scribner's Sons, New York, 1905. Reissued by Singing Trees Press, Book Tower, Detroit. 1968.

Sumner, W. L. The Organ. Third Edition, Macdonald and Co. Ltd. London. 1964.

Jackson, Sir Thomas Graham. Gothic Architecture Vol. I. University of Chicago Press. Chicago, 1915.

Edwards, George Wharton. Vanished Halls and Cathedrals of France. Penn Publishing Company, Philadelphia. 1917.

Aelred, Saint, Abbot of Rievaulx. Speculum Caritatis (Liber II)—The Mirror of Charity. (British Museum) Translated with introduction and notes by Geoffrey Webb and Adrian Walker. Mowbray and Company, London, 1962.

d'Aquin, Pierre-Louis. Siècle Littéraire de Louis XV. Duchesne, Amsterdam, 1754. 8°.

Tessier, A. L'Oeuvres de clavecin de Nicholas le Bègue in Revue de Musicologie, August, 1923.

Tessier, A. Un exemplaire original des pieces d'orgue de Couperin in Revue de Musicologie, May, 1929.

Gastoué, A. Notes complementaires sur une copie de la "Messe solennelle" de Couperin in Revue de Musicologie, May, 1929.

Bouvet, Charles. Les Deux d'Anglebert et Marquerite-Antoine Couperin in Revue de Musicologie, May, 1928.

Raugel, Félix. The Ancient French Organ School (Paris 1636-1637: Vault ML 100-M574) in the Musical Quarterly, 1925. Vol. XI, No. 3. Reprinted 1968. AMS Press, Inc. New York, New York. 10003

Mennesson, Em. (éditeur, Reims) Revue musicale Sainte-Cécile, 7 juillet, 1892.

Lettres de Peiresc. t, VII pp. 588 to 590. Published by Ph. Tamizey de Larroque, 1898.

Quittard, Henri. Notes sur G. Machaut et son oeuvre (Fin.) in Bulletin de la Société Française de Musicologie, Librairie Félix Alcan. Paris, 1918 (Dec.)

Zwick, Gabriel. Deux Motets inédits de Phillipe de Vitry et de Guillaume de Machaut in Revue de Musicologie, 1948-50, p. 28.

le Cerf, G. Notes sur le clavicorde et le dulce melos du ms. Lat. 7295 in Revue de Musicologie, Feb. 1931, p. 99.

Gastoué, A. A propos de Quelques organistes de l'église Saint-Gervais avant les Couperins—Les Du Buisson in Revue de Musicologie, 1930, p. 241.

Cauchie, Maurice. Documents pour servir à une biographie de Guillaume Costeley in Revue de Musicologie, May, 1926.

Droz, Eugene. Les Chansons de Nicholas de la Grotte in Revue de Musicologie, August, 1927.

Tiersot, Julien. Une famille de musiciens français: les de la Barre in Revue de Musicologie, November, 1927 and May, 1928.

Gastoué, A. Notes sur la Généalogie et la Famille de l'organiste Titelouze (1563-1633) in Revue de Musicologie, 1930, p. 171.

Tessier, A. Une pièce d'orgue de Charles Raquet et le Mersenne de la Bibliothèque des Minimes de Paris in Revue de Musicologie, November, 1929.

Bouvet, Charles. Un musicien oublié: Charles Piroye in Revue de Musicologie, November, 1928.

Raugel, A. Les grandes orgues et les organistes de la basilique de Saint-Quentin, Argenteuil, 1925, pp. 36-44.

Dufourcq, Norbert. A travers l'inédit, Recherchers II, Contract de mariage de Nicolas de Grigny, Paris, 1962, p. 235.

Tribune de Saint Gervais. Traveux de l'Académie de Reims CXIII. 1905. (Nicolas de Grigny)

Jadart, M. H., Secrétaire Général. Communiques a l'Académie de Reims "Lettres de M. André Pirro" - 1903.

Travaux de l'Académie de Reims, t. XXV, p. 264; t. LXVII, p. 137; t. II, p. 217; t. LXXXIV, p. 233.

Registres paroissiaux de Reims—Documents sur la Famille de Grigny.

Registres—Paroisse Saint-Symphorien — f° 48 et f° 50 archives communales.

Registres—Paroisse Saint-Etienne 1670-1693.

Registres—Paroisse Saint-Michel 1703-1709.

Registres—Paroisse Saint-Denis 1718.

Attaingnant, Pierre. Deux Livres d'Orgue. Publication de la Société Française de Musicologie, Tome I, E. Droz, Paris, 1925.

Guilmant, Alexandre and Pirro, André, editors. Archives des Maîtres de l'Orgue du XVIe, XVIIe, et XVIIIe Siècles, Vols. I, II, III, IV, V, VI. A. Durand et Fils, Paris 1898-1904. (Microfilm, Library of Congress, Washington, D.C.)

Couperin, F. Musique d'Orgue. Oiseau-Lyre, Paris, 1932.

Raugel, Félix. Les Maîtres Français de l'Orgue aux XVIIe et XVIIe Siècles. Editions Musicales de la Schola Cantorem, Paris, 1951.

Gay, Harry W. French Organ Music 1549-1756. St. Mary's Press. New York, 1958.

de Grigny, Nicholas. Livre d'Orgue. Edition of Christophe Ballard, 1711. Bibliothèque Nationale, Vol. 1834.

de Grigny, Nicholas. First Book for the Organ (1700). Royal Library, London.

Anthologie des Maîtres classique de l'Orgue (Revisions by Marcel Dupré) S. Bornemann, Paris, 1942 et suiv.

Les Grand Organistes français du XVIIe et du XVIIIe siècles (Revision by G. Jacob) Paris. Procure Générale.

Bonnet, Joseph. An Anthology of Early French Organ Music. H. W. Gray Co. Inc. (Now Belwin-Mills). New York. 1942.

Bonnet, Joseph. Historical Organ Recitals—Series I. G. Schirmer, New York. 1917 and 1945.

Vogan, Charles Edward. French Organ School of the 17th and 18th Century. 1948. 2 vols., microfilm. University of Michigan, Ann Arbor, Michigan. (University Microfilm 1358).

Organ Tablatures. (Lüneburg) Mss. K.N. 147. 146 frames in 28 strips. Indiana University, Bloomington, Indiana.

Besard, Jean Baptiste. Thesaurus harmonius. 1603. Isham Library, Harvard University, Cambridge, Massachusetts.

Organ Fantasies. British Museum. Ms. additional 15233, fol. 1-10. Isham Library, Harvard University, Cambridge, Massachusetts.

Organ Pieces. British Museum. Ms. additional 17852, fol. 4-10, 94. Isham Library, Harvard University, Cambridge, Massachusetts.

Charpentier, Marc Antoine. Elévation pour un dessus deux violins et l'orgue. University of Michigan, Ann Arbor, Michigan. Antiene (pour flûte, violin et orgue). University of Michigan, Ann Arbor, Michigan. Offerte pour l'orgue et pour les violins, flûtes et hautbois. University of Michigan. Ann Arbor, Michigan.

Charpentier, Jean J. B. Douze noëls varies pour l'orgue avec un carillon des morts. Oeuvres XIIIe, Paris, Le Duc. Also University of Michigan, Ann Arbor, Michigan. Journal d'orgue a l'usage des paroisses et communantes religieuse. No. 2. Paris, Chez Le Duc. University of Michigan, Ann Arbor, Michigan.

Droz, Eugene (éditeur). Trois chansonniers français du XVe siècle. Paris, E. Droz, 1927. (Documents artistiques du XVe siècle. t. 4). Microfilm—University of California at Berkeley.

Duphly (Duflitz). Pièces de clavecin. Livre 1-4. Paris 17—. Isham Library. Harvard University, Cambridge, Massachusetts.

Jullien, Gilles. Premier livre d'orgue. Paris, Richar 1690. University of Michigan, Ann Arbor, Michigan.

Royer, Pièces de clavecin. 1er livre. Paris, 1746. Isham Library, Harvard University, Cambridge, Massachusetts.

de Laborde, M. le Marquis. Chansonnier de M. le Marquis de Laborde. U.S. Library of Congress, Division of Music. Music microfilm archive 108. Film of photographs of original 15th century manuscript.

Valois, Philippe. Trio for the organ or the clavecin. Paris, Berault. University of Michigan, Ann Arbor, Michigan.

Index